Daniel Decoded: Deciphering Bible Prophecy

Brian Johnston

Published by Hayes Press, 2016.

Published by

HAYES PRESS CHRISTIAN RESOURCES

The Barn, Flaxlands

Royal Wootton Bassett

Swindon, SN4 8DY

United Kingdom

www.hayespress.org

Copyright © 2016 HAYES PRESS

If you enjoyed reading this book and/or others in the series, we would really appreciate it if you could just take a couple of minutes to leave a brief online review.

As a thank-you for purchasing this book, please help yourself to a free download of "Healthy Churches – God's Bible Blueprint For Growth" by Brian Johnston in the Search For Truth Series:

Amazon.com: http://amzn.to/1FuoN5l

Amazon.co.uk: http://amzn.to/1HTSize

TABLE OF CONTENTS

CHAPTER ONE: MIGRANTS, AN ALIEN CULTURE & A HAM SANDWICH

More than 4.5 million refugees from Syria are spread across five countries today. But we begin this book on Daniel with a look at a migrant crisis which occurred more than two and a half thousand years ago. Daniel and his compatriots were not merely migrants; they were deportees, forced out of their homeland by the then world superpower of the Babylonian empire. Not the best way to begin to experience international travel. Here's how the Old Testament book known as the book of Daniel opens:

"In the third year of the reign of Jehoiakim king of Judah, Nebuchadnezzar king of Babylon came to Jerusalem and besieged it. The Lord gave Jehoiakim king of Judah into his hand, along with some of the vessels of the house of God; and he brought them to the land of Shinar, to the house of his god, and he brought the vessels into the treasury of his god. Then the king ordered Ashpenaz, the chief of his officials, to bring in some of the sons of Israel, including some of the royal family and of the nobles, in whom was no defect, who were good-looking, showing intelligence in every branch of wisdom, endowed with understanding and discerning knowledge, and who had ability for serving in the king's court; and he ordered him to teach them the literature and language of the Chaldeans" (Daniel 1:1-4).

A lot of people deny there can be a good God if bad stuff happens to them, but Daniel was in another league altogether. Even although he knew the calamitous changing of his world, we'll find he remained loyal to his beliefs and was even later described as the object of God's delight or desire in the Bible book that goes by his name. It seems we'd be justified in viewing Daniel as an example of 'the person whose happiness God desires' – which is a way of translating a phrase repeatedly used to describe Daniel in the Bible (see Daniel 9:23; 10:11; 10:19; literally 'man of desirability'). What marks Daniel out for such honourable mention? We'll learn to view Daniel as a person of immense integrity who was capable, by God's help, of withstanding colossal pressure without compromising his principles.

The book in the Bible bearing Daniel's name, and which tells us his story, is a book of two halves: the first half contains some of those wonderful adventures he experienced, and which we may have learned about in Sunday School as children; but the second half is a mysterious and difficult section full of wonderful prophetic messages of worldwide and end-time importance. Both sections are equally fascinating, and so let's look forward to unpacking them together.

As we've hinted, here we find prophecy birthed in difficult times. In fact, both the Bible books of Daniel and Revelation set their prophetic content within a historical context that was very challenging to belief. Both Daniel and John were exiled for their faith, one in Babylon, the other in Patmos. Each human author of these prophetic books first proved himself trustworthy of the insight which God gave him to share with us. And the content of their respective visions fit together to give a coherent message which is very meaningful for today, as I hope we'll see.

So, let's begin by thinking of the hostile environment for faith which Daniel found himself transported into when the Babylonians overran his native land of Israel and city of Jerusalem, and transported him far from home. In this way, Daniel was suddenly exposed to radically different thinking compared with all he'd been brought up to know. What's more, he was now immersed in a culture that was intolerant of alternatives. As a young man, Daniel found himself catapulted into a kind of hostile environment which we can increasingly relate to in the modern western world. Nebuchadnezzar was the most powerful sovereign ever to rule the world, and was someone who at times exuded the misplaced confidence that God didn't exist.

The corridors of power, the entire education system, and whatever mass media existed then, were all filled with a kind of thinking that was radically different to that of Daniel, and the three close companions who'd been taken alongside him, and who also get honourable mention in the pages of the book. There's a lot we can learn from them about engaging with culture but without diluting our principles. It's as if Daniel can be compared to a young student removed from his or her sheltered home environment and no longer accountable to parents or any previous religious teaching and upbringing. Here was a chance for Daniel to break free from all that if he wanted to. Or, alternatively, here was an opportunity to swim against the flow and witness to God's truth and bring glory to God's name.

It was a world then – like now - which squeezed everything into its mould (Romans 12:2), and didn't tolerate alternative views – just like we face with regard to say, origins science and sexual ethics. Daniel and the other young nobles who'd been singled out for special treatment were put on a fast-track learning program to get to grips with the different language and worldview of the Babylonians. Here's what we read in Daniel chapter 1:

"The king appointed for them a daily ration from the king's choice food and from the wine which he drank, and appointed that they should be educated three years, at the end of which they were to enter the king's personal service. Now among them from the sons of Judah were Daniel, Hananiah, Mishael and Azariah. Then the commander of the officials assigned new names to them; and to Daniel he assigned the name Belteshazzar, to Hananiah

Shadrach, to Mishael Meshach and to Azariah Abed-nego. But Daniel made up his mind that he would not defile himself with the king's choice food or with the wine which he drank; so he sought permission from the commander of the officials that he might not defile himself.

Now God granted Daniel favor and compassion in the sight of the commander of the officials, and the commander of the officials said to Daniel, "I am afraid of my lord the king, who has appointed your food and your drink; for why should he see your faces looking more haggard than the youths who are your own age? Then you would make me forfeit my head to the king." But Daniel said to the overseer whom the commander of the officials had appointed over Daniel, Hananiah, Mishael and Azariah, "Please test your servants for ten days, and let us be given some vegetables to eat and water to drink. Then let our appearance be observed in your presence and the appearance of the youths who are eating the king's choice food; and deal with your servants according to what you see." So he listened to them in this matter and tested them for ten days" (Daniel 1:5-14).

Daniel nailed his colours to the mast straightaway, as we say – in other words, he began as he intended to continue. Here was a man whose native land had been over-run in his youth, now he was a deportee in a foreign culture, and confronting the greatest autocrat ever. Should he go with the flow? After all, what more was there to lose? Why not succumb to situational ethics and do whatever it takes to survive in desperate times? After all, those who'd previously taught him differently were no longer there to check on him.

But Daniel even rejects a ham sandwich, when there was no-one to criticise him for eating it! You laugh – meaning you think it was no big deal? Then you're not a Daniel! Now, I know the Bible doesn't specify it was a ham sandwich – or even the pork that was forbidden for a Jew to eat. In fact, the issue troubling Daniel could well have been a worry about whether the food he was being offered had previously been part of some pagan idolatrous ritual. But, if you'll bear with me, the somewhat light-hearted reference to a ham sandwich helps me to make the point that, down to that level of detail, Daniel's beliefs were convictions not preferences; in the small matter of the ham sandwich (or whatever it was), we're introduced in Daniel chapter 1 to a man of integrity who in the battle for ideas was quite prepared to take on the world.

"At the end of ten days their appearance seemed better and they were fatter than all the youths who had been eating the king's choice food. So the overseer continued to withhold their choice food and the wine they were to drink, and kept giving them vegetables. As for these four youths, God gave them knowledge and intelligence in every branch of literature and wisdom; Daniel even understood all kinds of visions and dreams. Then at the end of the days which the king had specified for presenting them, the commander of the officials presented them before Nebuchadnezzar. The king talked with them, and out of them all not one was found like Daniel, Hananiah, Mishael and Azariah; so they entered the king's personal service. As for every matter of wisdom and understanding about which the king consulted them, he found them ten times better than all the magicians and conjurers who were in all his realm. And Daniel continued until the first year of Cyrus the king" (Daniel 1:15-21).

The United Nations has defined a preference as something you believe in which you would be prepared to change your mind about under the pressure of changed circumstances. Whereas, they distinguish a conviction as a much stronger belief: one we're not prepared to change for anything under any circumstances. We've learned which kind Daniel's beliefs were, but would we say our beliefs are preferences or convictions? And, based on the life of Daniel, which kind of belief pleases and honours God?

CHAPTER ONE STUDY QUESTIONS

1. In what specific ways does Daniel in Babylon simulate a Christian within modern secular society?
2. Where do you find your particular environment (office, home, university, career structure, business ethics ...) to be most hostile to your Christian faith?
3. Was Daniel right to make such a big deal about such a 'small thing'? What kind of "small things" really matter to God today?
4. Do you find it strange that God should give Daniel and his friends understanding of "all kinds of literature and learning" (presumably pagan) – what do you take from that?
5. Reflecting on it, give evidence to support the claim that your beliefs are actually convictions rather than preferences.

CHAPTER TWO: GOD'S MAN COMES THROUGH

So far, we've thought of Daniel as a migrant, forced away from his sheltered and privileged upbringing and plunged into a totally foreign culture – one which was attempting to make him rethink everything he stood for. At points in our lives – albeit in much less extreme ways – we'll be forced either to stand on our own feet for what we've believed in or allow ourselves to be swept away with the new ideas of others.

But Daniel's original framework of beliefs was firmly Bible-based. He's therefore a role model to succeeding generations of what it means to stand up for God's truth when under extreme pressure to conform to a lesser or different standard. History has often repeated itself, for example around the turn of the 20th century when the world heard, and later tried to implement, the godless philosophy of Nietsche. When the scaffold of biblical values is removed from around society, will the righteous still stand as individuals? Daniel did at a time when Nebuchadnezzar was bossing the world.

This world ruler, Nebuchadnezzar, head of the mighty Babylonian empire in the 6th century BC, was not only incomparably powerful, but he was really smart, too. If you thought he was an absent-minded incompetent who forgot his own dreams then you've got the wrong man. Here's your chance to rethink that assessment as we quote from the second chapter of the book of Daniel:

"Now in the second year of the reign of Nebuchadnezzar, Nebuchadnezzar had dreams; and his spirit was troubled and his sleep left him. Then the king gave orders to call in the magicians, the conjurers, the sorcerers and the Chaldeans to tell the king his dreams. So they came in and stood before the king. The king said to them, 'I had a dream and my spirit is anxious to understand the dream.' Then the Chaldeans spoke to the king in Aramaic: ... 'Let the king tell the dream to his servants, and we will declare the interpretation.' The king replied, 'I know for certain that you are bargaining for time, inasmuch as you have seen that the command from me is firm, that if you do not make the dream known to me, there is only one decree for you. For you have agreed together to speak lying and corrupt words before me until the situation is changed; therefore tell me the dream, that I may know that you can declare to me its interpretation'" (Daniel 2:1-10).

Isn't it clear? This wasn't forgetfulness, but Nebuchadnezzar was behaving very shrewdly. If his advisors couldn't inform him what his dream had been why should he have any confidence they weren't simply also making up any old fanciful and flattering interpretation? So, Nebuchadnezzar was shrewd. Oh, and did I mention he was ruthless - for as we've just heard, he authorises the execution of all the intelligensia if they failed to comply with his request. Let's read on to capture the understandable reaction of his advisors:

"The Chaldeans answered the king and said, 'There is not a man on earth who could declare the matter for the king, inasmuch as no great king or ruler has ever asked anything like this of any magician, conjurer or Chaldean. Moreover, the thing which the king demands is difficult, and there is no one else who could declare it to the king except gods, whose dwelling place is not with mortal flesh.' Because of this the king became indignant and very furious and gave orders to destroy all the wise men of Babylon. So the decree went forth that the wise men should be slain; and they looked for Daniel and his friends to kill them.

Then Daniel replied with discretion and discernment to Arioch, the captain of the king's bodyguard, who had gone forth to slay the wise men of Babylon; he said to Arioch, the king's commander, 'For what reason is the decree from the king so urgent?' Then Arioch informed Daniel about the matter. So Daniel went in and requested of the king that he would give him time, in order that he might declare the interpretation to the king. Then Daniel went to his house and informed his friends, Hananiah, Mishael and Azariah, about the matter, so that they might request compassion from the God of heaven concerning this mystery, so that Daniel and his friends would not be destroyed with the rest of the wise men of Babylon" (Daniel 2:10-18).

This is some test, a real tight spot, with perhaps only 24 hours to live. The pressure on young Daniel was immense. At once Daniel takes it to the Lord in prayer, and requests his companions to do the same.

"Then the mystery was revealed to Daniel in a night vision. Then Daniel blessed the God of heaven; Daniel said, "Let the name of God be blessed forever and ever, ... "It is He who reveals the profound and hidden things; He knows what is in the darkness, And the light dwells with Him. "To You, O God of my fathers, I give thanks and praise, for You have given me wisdom and power; even now You have made known to me what we requested of You, for You have made known to us the king's matter" (Daniel 2:19-23).

Daniel is a man who knows his God, and God's man comes through. And we learn that if you're in touch with God, you can withstand the full brunt of the power of a society or a culture, or even an empire.

"Therefore, Daniel went in to Arioch, whom the king had appointed to destroy the wise men of Babylon; he went and spoke to him as follows: 'Do not destroy the wise men of Babylon! Take me into the king's presence, and I will declare the interpretation to the king.' Then Arioch hurriedly brought Daniel into the king's presence and spoke to him as follows: "I have found a man among the exiles from Judah who can make the interpretation known to the king!' The king said to Daniel, whose name was Belteshazzar, 'Are you able to make known to me the dream which I have seen and its interpretation?' Daniel answered before the king and said, 'As for the mystery about which the king has inquired, neither wise men, conjurers, magicians nor diviners are able to declare it to the king.'

'However, there is a God in heaven who reveals mysteries, and He has made known to King Nebuchadnezzar what will take place in the latter days. This was your dream and the visions in your mind while on your bed. As for you, O king, while on your bed your thoughts turned to what would take place in the future; and He who reveals mysteries has made known to you what will take place. But as for me, this mystery has not been revealed to me for any wisdom residing in me more than in any other living man, but for the purpose of making the interpretation known to the king, and that you may understand the thoughts of your mind. You, O king, were looking and behold, there was a single great statue; that statue, which was large and of extraordinary splendor, was standing in front of you, and its appearance was awesome.

'The head of that statue was made of fine gold, its breast and its arms of silver, its belly and its thighs of bronze, its legs of iron, its feet partly of iron and partly of clay. You continued looking until a stone was cut out without hands, and it struck the statue on its feet of iron and clay and crushed them. Then the iron, the clay, the bronze, the silver and the gold were crushed all at the same time and became like chaff from the summer threshing floors; and the wind carried them away so that not a trace of them was found. But the stone that struck the statue became a great mountain and filled the whole earth'" (Daniel 2:24-35).

Nebuchadnezzar would have instantly recognised his own dream, and that would have convinced him that the interpretation about to be shared now by Daniel was authentic.

"'This was the dream; now we will tell its interpretation before the king. You, O king, are the king of kings, to whom the God of heaven has given the kingdom, the power, the strength and the glory ... You are the head of gold. After you there will arise another kingdom inferior to you, then another third kingdom of bronze, which will rule over all the earth. Then there will be a fourth kingdom as strong as iron; inasmuch as iron crushes and shatters all things, so, like iron that breaks in pieces, it will crush and break all these in pieces. In that you saw the feet and toes, partly of potter's clay and partly of iron, it will be a divided kingdom; but it will have in it the toughness of iron, inasmuch as you saw the iron mixed with common clay ...

In the days of those kings the God of heaven will set up a kingdom which will never be destroyed, and that kingdom will not be left for another people; it will crush and put an end to all these kingdoms, but it will itself endure forever. Inasmuch as you saw that a stone was cut out of the mountain without hands and that it crushed the iron, the bronze, the clay, the silver and the gold, the great God has made known to the king what will take place in the future; so the dream is true and its interpretation is trustworthy" (Daniel 2:36-41,44-45).

Through Daniel, God revealed in the 6th century BC that from that time until the end-time only four kingdoms or empires would come to dominate the world centred on the Middle East. By chapter 8, we're additionally given names for the second and third empires which followed on from the Babylonian: they were the Medo-Persian and the Greek empires, respectively. The fourth empire is left un-named in the Bible. The usual view has been that it refers to the Roman empire which, however, was more Mid-European than Middle Eastern. Later, we'll explore if it could be possible that the Islamic State (or ISIS or Islamic Caliphate) is a better contender for Daniel's fourth world empire – one which we see re-emerging today.

We'll learn that this book of Daniel is amazingly up to date and relevant for our times. For now, however, our main and simple lesson has been to see and learn from the close, habitual relationship Daniel had with God through prayer, and the confidence which that gave him to trust in God in a crisis - and what's more to have a real boldness in communicating God's message. Do we have anything remotely like that calibre of relationship with God, and with it the boldness to declare to others God's message which we discover by the Spirit in the Bible for us today?

CHAPTER TWO STUDY QUESTIONS

1. What's the most dramatic answer to prayer you've experienced?
2. List some of the ways in which Daniel is a helpful role model for prayer in this chapter.
3. Do you think Daniel was tempted to take the credit for interpreting the dream, rather than give the glory to God?
4. Can you think of other times that God sometimes gives the greatest of revelations to the most unlikely of people, like Nebuchadnezzar?
5. Do events in the world as they are taking shape today influence you one way or another in attempting to identify the fourth world empire which Daniel intriguingly left unspecified?

CHAPTER THREE: THE WORLD'S HOTTEST FIRE

What's the ultimate in peer pressure you've had to withstand? Someone said to me recently, 'dead fish go with the flow, those that are alive have a choice.' With new life in Jesus, we don't need to go with the flow. Indeed, since the world system in terms of its values and beliefs and ideas is held in the grip of the Devil - which is what the Bible (in 1 John 5:19) tells us – then it follows that we need to be swimming against its current of opinion. The Apostle John tells us that if we love this world with its polluted moral atmosphere, then the love of God the Father is not in us (1 John 2:14-15).

Some two and a half thousand years ago, three men who were companions of Daniel, were put to the test. The law of their God, given some one thousand years earlier, strictly warned them against worshiping any image or idol. None other than the true God of heaven was to be the object of their worship, and not even a representation of him in the form of any created thing was acceptable in facilitating that worship. Anything we can manufacture reduces God to our likeness; whereas the reality is it's the other way around – we, as humans, were made in God's likeness – not physically, but as relational and rational and moral beings, capable of ruling and being creative, and above all designed for fellowship with our Maker.

But let's get back to Daniel's three friends, and what was surely to become the biggest adventure of their lives. You'll remember they are prisoners of war, prisoners who've been re-educated and assimilated into the culture of the Babylonian empire – or at least

that was the king's intention, for he evidently viewed them as
young people of real potential. So we read:

"Nebuchadnezzar the king made an image of gold, the height of
which was sixty cubits and its width six cubits; he set it up on the
plain of Dura in the province of Babylon. Then the satraps, the
prefects and the governors, the counselors, the treasurers, the
judges, the magistrates and all the rulers of the provinces were
assembled for the dedication of the image that Nebuchadnezzar
the king had set up; and they stood before the image that
Nebuchadnezzar had set up. Then the herald loudly proclaimed:
'To you the command is given, O peoples, nations and men of
every language, that at the moment you hear the sound of the
horn, flute, lyre, trigon, psaltery, bagpipe and all kinds of music,
you are to fall down and worship the golden image that
Nebuchadnezzar the king has set up. But whoever does not fall
down and worship shall immediately be cast into the midst of a
furnace of blazing fire.' Therefore at that time, when all the
peoples heard the sound of the horn, flute, lyre, trigon, psaltery,
bagpipe and all kinds of music, all the peoples, nations and men of
every language fell down and worshiped the golden image that
Nebuchadnezzar the king had set up" (Daniel 3:1,3-7).

The command and the choice were equally clear. Not much of a
choice, was it? Faced with the world's most powerful man, the
world's hottest fire, and maybe even the world's loudest band ... the
entire population falls to their knees. Err, not quite all. All except
for three persons.

"For this reason at that time certain Chaldeans came forward
and brought charges against the Jews. 'There are certain Jews
whom you have appointed over the administration of the province
of Babylon, namely Shadrach, Meshach and Abed-nego. These
men, O king, have disregarded you; they do not serve your gods or
worship the golden image which you have set up.' Then

Nebuchadnezzar in rage and anger gave orders to bring Shadrach, Meshach and Abed-nego; then these men were brought before the king.

Nebuchadnezzar responded and said to them, 'Is it true, Shadrach, Meshach and Abed-nego, that you do not serve my gods or worship the golden image that I have set up? Now if you are ready, at the moment you hear the sound of the horn, flute, lyre, trigon, psaltery and bagpipe and all kinds of music, to fall down and worship the image that I have made, very well. But if you do not worship, you will immediately be cast into the midst of a furnace of blazing fire; and what god is there who can deliver you out of my hands?" (Daniel 3:8, 12-15).

Here we are about to see a vital spiritual law demonstrated, one that will again be required for the prophetic times lying ahead when those who know their God will once again need to perform such exploits as we're about to read of now (Daniel 11:32). Only those who know and serve God with real conviction could undertake what we're told happened next:

"Shadrach, Meshach and Abed-nego replied to the king, 'O Nebuchadnezzar, we do not need to give you an answer concerning this matter. If it be so, our God whom we serve is able to deliver us from the furnace of blazing fire; and He will deliver us out of your hand, O king. But even if He does not, let it be known to you, O king, that we are not going to serve your gods or worship the golden image that you have set up.' Then Nebuchadnezzar was filled with wrath, and his facial expression was altered toward Shadrach, Meshach and Abed-nego. He answered by giving orders to heat the furnace seven times more than it was usually heated.

He commanded certain valiant warriors who were in his army to tie up Shadrach, Meshach and Abed-nego in order to cast them into the furnace of blazing fire. Then these men were tied up in their trousers, their coats, their caps and their other clothes, and were cast into the midst of the furnace of blazing fire. For this reason, because the king's command was urgent and the furnace had been made extremely hot, the flame of the fire slew those men who carried up Shadrach, Meshach and Abed-nego. But these three men, Shadrach, Meshach and Abed-nego, fell into the midst of the furnace of blazing fire still tied up" (Daniel 3:16-23).

Before we read about the outcome, allow me to quote the verses later in Daniel which I made reference to above. The following words are taken from Daniel chapter 11:32-33. "The people who know their God will [1] display strength and [2] take action. Those who [3] have insight among the people will [4] give understanding to the many.' I think this description is fully realized in the case of the three men who were Daniel's companions. Like Daniel, they knew their God. Such people, we've just discovered, have four characteristics – they display strength, they take action, they have insight, and they give understanding or show discernment.

The first listed characteristic is to 'be strong, take courage, behave valiantly.' In other words: "... to have great <u>boldness</u> for God." The second feature is they 'accomplish, are busy or industrious.' In other words: "... to have great <u>energy</u> for God." The third distinguishing feature is 'being circumspect, having comprehension.' In other words: "... to have great <u>thoughts</u> of God." And the fourth and last hallmark is 'to have discernment' e.g. of the type shown in trial by our three friends before Nebuchadnezzar. In some specialized sense then: "... to have great <u>contentment</u> in God." For these men were content to fall into the hands of the living God, content for his will to be done as to whether they lived or not, for they discerned that – whatever might happen – obeying God was best. For them, it was a no-brainer, as we might say. Okay, so what happened to the three friends? We read on …

"Then Nebuchadnezzar the king was astounded and stood up in haste; he said to his high officials, 'Was it not three men we cast bound into the midst of the fire?' They replied to the king, 'Certainly, O king.' He said, 'Look! I see four men loosed and walking about in the midst of the fire without harm, and the appearance of the fourth is like a son of the gods!' Then Nebuchadnezzar came near to the door of the furnace of blazing fire; he responded and said, 'Shadrach, Meshach and Abed-nego, come out, you servants of the Most High God, and come here!'

Then Shadrach, Meshach and Abed-nego came out of the midst of the fire. The satraps, the prefects, the governors and the king's high officials gathered around and saw in regard to these men that the fire had no effect on the bodies of these men nor was the hair of their head singed, nor were their trousers damaged, nor had the smell of fire even come upon them. Nebuchadnezzar responded and said, 'Blessed be the God of Shadrach, Meshach and Abed-nego, who has sent His angel and delivered His servants who put their trust in Him, violating the king's command, and yielded up their bodies so as not to serve or worship any god except their own God.

Therefore I make a decree that any people, nation or tongue that speaks anything offensive against the God of Shadrach, Meshach and Abed-nego shall be torn limb from limb and their houses reduced to a rubbish heap, inasmuch as there is no other god who is able to deliver in this way.' Then the king caused Shadrach, Meshach and Abed-nego to prosper in the province of Babylon" (Daniel 3:24-30).

Once again it's proved that God knows how to deliver the godly out of trial or temptation. And whenever there is such godly subjection to him, and his will, as that shown by these men, God is greatly glorified, as was most definitely the case here. Now, the application of this to our lives may be: am I facing some crisis of conscience; am I caught on the horns of some ethical dilemma; am I debating with myself if continuing to serve God by sticking to my Bible-based convictions is really worth it? Then I hope you have heard the answer of God's Word, and may you live out what it means to truly know God: to think highly of God, to be bold and energetic for his cause, and content to discern that his will is best. And let's remember to pray for brothers and sisters in Christ who in some parts of the world today really are facing the heat.

CHAPTER THREE STUDY QUESTIONS

1. When have you found yourself up against peer pressure? How do you think you coped?
2. What "idols of gold" are we, as Christians, under pressure to bow down to today?
3. What helped the three heroes of this chapter to pass their test with flying colours?
4. How might the 4 characteristics of 'those who know God' relate to other well-known Bible characters such as Moses, David or Paul?
5. Do you have any idea who the fourth figure in the fiery furnace may have been?
6. Nebuchadnezzar describes the three friends as servants of "the Most High God" – what is the significance of this title of God in the Old Testament and what does it tell us about Nebuchadnezzar's understanding of God?

CHAPTER FOUR: BECOMING BESTIAL

The Apostle Paul wrote telling Timothy by the Spirit of God that he should instruct those in the Church of God at Ephesus to pray for all people, including those in the highest offices in the land they lived in, as well as all who exercised political power over them regardless of how legitimate or otherwise it was (1 Timothy 2:1-2). He didn't require them to run their prayers through any kind of political censorship.

Recently, I was in a country that had democratically elected its new President. Shockingly, he'd previously joked about the rape and murder of a female missionary. Now he boasts he'll ignore human rights in the name of justice. Pray that by God's sovereign hand our brothers and sisters there - and all of good will - may experience the opportunity for godliness in tranquility. In whatever God permits, we must remember the Gospel is unhindered.

It's in the fourth chapter of Daniel's book that we have presented to us the life-changing testimony of a colossal leader of Empire: the colossus who was Nebuchadnezzar, perhaps the most powerful world leader who has ever exercised power. Not for nothing does the Bible record God's message to him as declaring that he was the head of gold. The metals representing successor empires would be progressively inferior. This man wasn't democratically elected. And he probably wasn't the sort of ruler you'd expect Christians to vote for anyway (that's if you believe it's right for Christians to vote – we'll come back to that controversial point). But whether he'd have got your vote or not, God had raised him to the highest office, not only in the land but in the world. But when he refused to acknowledge the true God, he became positively bestial. It's worth hearing what he's got to say from the top of Daniel chapter 4:

"Nebuchadnezzar the king to all the peoples, nations, and men of every language that live in all the earth: 'May your peace abound! It has seemed good to me to declare the signs and wonders which the Most High God has done for me. How great are His signs and how mighty are His wonders! His kingdom is an everlasting kingdom and His dominion is from generation to generation. I, Nebuchadnezzar, was at ease in my house and flourishing in my palace. I saw a dream and it made me fearful; and these fantasies as I lay on my bed and the visions in my mind kept alarming me. So I gave orders to bring into my presence all the wise men of Babylon, that they might make known to me the interpretation of the dream. Then the magicians, the conjurers, the Chaldeans and the diviners came in and I related the dream to them, but they could not make its interpretation known to me.

But finally Daniel came in before me, whose name is Belteshazzar according to the name of my god, and in whom is a spirit of the holy gods; and I related the dream to him, saying,

'O Belteshazzar, chief of the magicians, since I know that a spirit of the holy gods is in you and no mystery baffles you, tell me the visions of my dream which I have seen, along with its interpretation. Now these were the visions in my mind as I lay on my bed: I was looking, and behold, there was a tree in the midst of the earth and its height was great. The tree grew large and became strong and its height reached to the sky, and it was visible to the end of the whole earth. Its foliage was beautiful and its fruit abundant, and in it was food for all. The beasts of the field found shade under it, And the birds of the sky dwelt in its branches, and all living creatures fed themselves from it.

I was looking in the visions in my mind as I lay on my bed, and behold, an angelic watcher, a holy one, descended from heaven. He shouted out and spoke as follows: 'Chop down the tree and cut off its branches, strip off its foliage and scatter its fruit; Let the beasts flee from under it and the birds from its branches. Yet leave the stump with its roots in the ground, but with a band of iron and bronze around it in the new grass of the field; And let him be drenched with the dew of heaven, and let him share with the beasts in the grass of the earth. Let his mind be changed from that of a man and let a beast's mind be given to him, and let seven periods of time pass over him. This sentence is by the decree of the angelic watchers and the decision is a command of the holy ones, in order that the living may know **that the Most High is ruler over the realm of mankind, and bestows it on whom He wishes and sets over it the lowliest of men.**'

'This is the dream which I, King Nebuchadnezzar, have seen. Now you, Belteshazzar, tell me its interpretation, inasmuch as none of the wise men of my kingdom is able to make known to me the interpretation; but you are able, for a spirit of the holy gods is in you.' Then Daniel, whose name is Belteshazzar, was appalled for a while as his thoughts alarmed him. The king responded and said, 'Belteshazzar, do not let the dream or its interpretation alarm you.' Belteshazzar replied, 'My lord, if only the dream applied to those who hate you and its interpretation to your adversaries!

The tree that you saw, which became large and grew strong, whose height reached to the sky and was visible to all the earth and whose foliage was beautiful and its fruit abundant, and in which was food for all, under which the beasts of the field dwelt and in whose branches the birds of the sky lodged - it is you, O king; for you have become great and grown strong, and your majesty has become great and reached to the sky and your dominion to the end of the earth.

In that the king saw an angelic watcher, a holy one, descending from heaven and saying, 'Chop down the tree and destroy it; yet leave the stump with its roots in the ground, but with a band of iron and bronze around it in the new grass of the field, and let him be drenched with the dew of heaven, and let him share with the beasts of the field until seven periods of time pass over him', this is the interpretation, O king, and this is the decree of the Most High, which has come upon my lord the king: that you be driven away from mankind and your dwelling place be with the beasts of the field, and you be given grass to eat like cattle and be drenched with the dew of heaven; and seven periods of time will pass over you, until you recognize that the Most High is ruler over the realm of mankind and bestows it on whomever He wishes.

And in that it was commanded to leave the stump with the roots of the tree, your kingdom will be assured to you after you recognize that it is Heaven that rules. Therefore, O king, may my advice be pleasing to you: break away now from your sins by doing righteousness and from your iniquities by showing mercy to the poor, in case there may be a prolonging of your prosperity.' All this happened to Nebuchadnezzar the king" (Daniel 4:1-28).

But through the witness of Daniel, God changed him and brought him to acknowledge the thesis of the entire book of Daniel - that the Most High rules in the kingdoms of men (Daniel 4:24-6). Here it is in his own words:

"But at the end of that period, I, Nebuchadnezzar, raised my eyes toward heaven and my reason returned to me, and I blessed the Most High and praised and honored Him who lives forever; For His dominion is an everlasting dominion, and His kingdom endures from generation to generation. All the inhabitants of the earth are accounted as nothing, but He does according to His will in the host of heaven and among the inhabitants of earth; and no one can ward off His hand or say to Him, 'What have You done?'

At that time my reason returned to me. And my majesty and splendor were restored to me for the glory of my kingdom, and my counselors and my nobles began seeking me out; so I was re-established in my sovereignty, and surpassing greatness was added to me. Now I, Nebuchadnezzar, praise, exalt and honor the King of heaven, for all His works are true and His ways just, and He is able to humble those who walk in pride" (Daniel 4:34-37).

God had raised up the basest of men, and God had also humbled this ruler of men who walked in pride. He was someone with whom God did business, but who – of all God-fearing people – would have voted for this man if they'd have had the option (which they didn't have then, of course)? The ballot box cannot thwart God's sovereign - and at times to us inscrutable - purposes. In this instance, and in many others since, we'd likely have cast our vote and found ourselves to be opposing the will of God. Not for nothing do we hear Paul saying in his follow-up letter to Timothy in 2 Timothy 2:4: "No soldier in active service entangles himself in the affairs of everyday life, so that he may please the one who enlisted him as a soldier."

The best soldier of all was equally emphatic in his reply to Pontius Pilate: "Jesus answered, 'My kingdom is not of this world. If My kingdom were of this world, then My servants would be fighting so that I would not be handed over to the Jews; but as it is, My kingdom is not of this realm'" (John 18:36).

How vital it is that we realize that our citizenship is in heaven (Philippians 3:20)! As far as possible in accordance with Biblical commands and principles, we're bound to be subject to earthly rulers (see Romans 13:1; Acts 5:29), but as the surrounding verses show, after a little thought, God has empowered our political masters with discharging a function which is expressly forbidden to the individual Christian. They are authorized by God to carry the sword of justice – and that not in vain (Romans 13:4) – but followers of Christ must not resist evil with evil (Romans 12:17). So it's not for us to become entangled with the political realm, not for us to attempt to second-guess God's inscrutable purposes via the ballot box.

Pray for our leaders, the Bible says. That, and no more. We're encouraged to relieve needs, but nowhere are told in the New Testament to campaign for social reforms (certainly not in 1 Peter). Instead, we're to demonstrate in God's Kingdom how subjection to the rule of God over his people promotes joy, peace and power in the Holy Spirit (Romans 14:17) - now that should be attractive to others in this sad world of war and injustice!

CHAPTER FOUR STUDY QUESTIONS

1. Does what happened to Nebuchadnezzar in this chapter remind you of a man that Jesus spoke about in Luke 12? How do these examples of being brought low help you to think differently about life, especially in view of Jesus' words in Matthew 23:12?
2. Why didn't Nebuchadnezzar repent when given the warning and the opportunity? Compare this to people who do not accept the gospel to escape God's judgement.
3. Do you think Christians should vote or become involved in politics? Give reasons.
4. Sincere Christians who vote often express diametrically opposed views. Does the chapter point to a better way? If you think it doesn't, explain why not.
5. Recalling the different stances taken on participation by Abraham and Lot regarding the cities of the plain, especially Sodom - Abraham prayed remotely while Lot participated in the city 'council' – whom did God use? Whose life was blessed and whose was adversely affected?

CHAPTER FIVE: LET THE CRITICS EAT THEIR WORDS

Belshazzar is called king several times in the Book of Daniel (Daniel 5:1,9,30;7:1;8:1). There may be many things we still don't know about the historical setting of Daniel, but we understand from Babylonian records that actually someone called Nabonidus was the king of Babylon at this time. Now the point is he's not mentioned by name in the Bible. So, following the Bible, how can it be said that Belshazzar is king? And in any case, why was Daniel – in chapter 5:16 - appointed as the third ruler in the kingdom (also see Daniel 5:7,16,29)? Why the third - who were the other two?

Few books of the Old Testament have come under such critical attack as Daniel. By post-dating the book and so claiming it was written after the events it predicted as occurring from the 6th century B.C. onwards, some of its prophetic statements have been relegated to mere historical footnotes. This is the view of liberal scholars, and raises the issue: 'Can we trust our Bibles?'

It turns out that we can, and let's use this 'Daniel challenge' as an example of how more careful historical and archeological and scientific research time after time ends up vindicating the Bible. An article by Dr. Alan R. Millard dealing with these issues appeared in Biblical Archaeology Review (May/June, 1985). At the time, Millard was a Senior Lecturer in Hebrew and Ancient Semitic Languages at the University of Liverpool, England. He explains there about the discovery of clay cylinders in southern Iraq by J. G. Taylor. A man called Sir Henry Rawlinson was able to read the Babylonian inscriptions on them which had been written at the command of Nabonidus, king of Babylon from 555 to 539 B.C. The words were a prayer for the long life and good health of Nabonidus - and for his eldest son. And the name of that son, clearly written, was Belshazzar!

Remember what we said earlier - the Bible book of Daniel has been one of the books unbelievers and critics have targetted most. One of their strongest arguments against it being genuine was in claiming that such a character as Belshazzar never existed – since, they thought, he was unknown to history. Historians were sure Nabonidus was the last Babylonian king, and that he was absent from the city when it was captured. The conclusion was the Belshazzar was mythical and the whole story of Daniel could be dismissed as legendary. However, that was before those clay cylinders were found at Chaldean sites which mentioned Belshazzar as being the eldest son of Nabonidus. Doubtless then, he reigned as regent in the city during his father's absences. This would have made him the second ruler (co-regent) in the kingdom and explains why he appointed Daniel as the third ruler in the kingdom (Daniel 5:16).

Here was clear proof that an important person named Belshazzar lived in Babylon during the last years of the city's independence. So Belshazzar was not an imaginary figure after all. In some of the inscriptions discovered from the reign of Nabonidus, we find that the parties swear by Nabonidus and by Belshazzar, the king's son. This suggests that Belshazzar may well have had a special status. We know that during part of his father's reign, Belshazzar was the effective authority in Babylon. According to one account, Nabonidus 'entrusted the kingship' to Belshazzar (BAR 11:03, May/June 1985). As Belshazzar was already second in the kingdom, serving as a co-regent with his absent father, he could offer Daniel nothing greater than to become 'third ruler in the kingdom.' Why should Daniel gain that honour? Well, with good reason now to trust the Bible account as factual, we join chapter 5 as it sets the scene for us.

Night is falling over the great capital of Babylon, with its buildings and towers and the Euphrates flowing through it. Here are the Hanging Gardens, built by Nebuchadnezzar for his bride, homesick on the flat Mesopotamian plains for the mountains of her native land. This is not just any night, for on this night there's to be a great banquet for Belshazzar and a thousand of his lords and nobles, their ladies, and his wives and concubines. Imagine a banqueting hall in keeping with the splendour of a world empire.

With the guests all seated, and the banquet underway, Belshazzar decides to startle his guests with an unheard-of performance: "He gave orders to bring in the gold and silver goblets that Nebuchadnezzar his father had taken from the temple in Jerusalem, so that the king and his nobles, his wives and his concubines might drink from them. Suddenly the fingers of a human hand appeared and wrote on the plaster of the wall, near the lampstand in the royal palace. The king watched the hand as it wrote. His face turned pale and he was so frightened that his knees knocked together and his legs gave way.

The king called out for the enchanters, astrologers and diviners to be brought and said to these wise men of Babylon, "Whoever reads this writing and tells me what it means will be clothed in purple and have a gold chain placed around his neck, and he will be made the third highest ruler in the kingdom." Then all the king's wise men came in, but they could not read the writing or tell the king what it meant. So King Belshazzar became even more terrified and his face grew more pale. His nobles were baffled" (Daniel 5:2-9 NIV).

What a grand defiance! What a royal joke, to drink to the health of the heathen gods - the gods of silver, gold, iron, brass,

wood, and stone - with the vessels dedicated to the worship of the
Most High God! Where was the God of the Hebrews? He was
nearer than anyone thought – as suddenly, over against the
lampstand, illuminated clearly by its light, the king saw to his
horror the fingers of a man's hand writing on the wall. His face
then drained of all colour and his knees began to knock. Mene,
Mene, Tekel, Parsin! Those were the words the fingers left behind
on the wall, but no one could read them. Then the queen
remembered the old Hebrew statesman who had served under
Nebuchadnezzar. The queen wasn't present at the banquet, for it
was hardly a fit place for her. But when the news was brought to
her of what had happened, she came in and told the king about
Daniel, who was able to give interpretations and to solve difficult
problems.

The king then gave an order that Daniel should be brought in,
and soon an old man made his appearance. What a contrast
between this Hebrew statesman and prophet and Belshazzar and
his revellers! As Daniel stood there, I imagine his strong God-
fearing countenance with its white locks surveying this spectacle of
debauchery - and recent hilarity - but now frozen in terror! Daniel
was candid as he gave the interpretation of the writing on the wall:

"'This is the inscription that was written: MENE, MENE,
TEKEL, PARSIN. This is what these words mean: Mene: God has
numbered the days of your reign and brought it to an end. Tekel:
You have been weighed on the scales and found wanting. Peres:
Your kingdom is divided and given to the Medes and Persians.'
Then at Belshazzar's command, Daniel was clothed in purple, a
gold chain was placed around his neck, and he was proclaimed the
third highest ruler in the kingdom. That very night Belshazzar,
king of the Babylonians, was slain, and Darius the Mede took over
the kingdom, at the age of sixty-two" (Daniel 5:25-31 NIV).

Belshazzar is an example of a man who refused to be taught and who wouldn't be warned. In that brief and powerful sermon, Daniel reminded the king of the pride and blasphemy of his predecessor upon the throne, Nebuchadnezzar, and how God had dealt with it. Yet, unwarned by that, Belshazzar had gone one worse than Nebuchadnezzar and had exalted himself to a climax of infamy and blasphemy by drinking wine out of the cups from the Jerusalem Temple. Note, please, that neither Belshazzar nor anyone else goes to his or her doom unwarned.

Belshazzar suddenly, on that night, saw a hand writing on the wall. It was writing his judgment and doom, the last chapter of his personal history (and of his empire). Nothing could now be changed, nothing altered. Weighed in the balance of his wives and concubines and the thousand revellers at his banquet that night, Belshazzar was not found wanting. His guests had surely been enjoying the grandeur and the debauchery of it all for, as Jesus said, people 'love the darkness'. But it's not the judgment and balance of this world that counts, but God's judgment and God's balance. Weighed in that balance, Belshazzar was found wanting.

And God weighs us in the balance. He's the searcher of every thought, the discerner of every secret, the observer of every act. All of us, weighed in his balance, searched by his judgment, are most definitely found wanting. But God has provided for us a weight of righteousness that's not our own. The apostle Paul said that God, "has wiped out the handwriting of requirements (or 'writing of the debt') that was against us, which was contrary to us. And He has taken it out of the way, having nailed it to the cross" (Colossians 2:14 NKJV).

Have you acknowledged, before a holy God, that as well as the writing on the cross that said; 'Jesus of Nazareth, King of the Jews'; there was other handwriting too – seen only by the eye of faith? Do you believe that the extent to which you've offended God was written there – nailed to the cross of Jesus – and it's as though God looked upon the death of his son there and then wrote 'Paid in Full' over the 'writing of the debt' – your debt.

But have you turned to God yet – and trusted for forgiveness in his son, Jesus Christ, the only Saviour? Again, may I ask you - when the hand begins to write, will it stop with that sentence, 'You are weighed in the balances, and found wanting'? or will it add, 'but found trusting in Christ'?

CHAPTER FIVE STUDY QUESTIONS

1. Have you ever doubted the historical accuracy of the Bible?
2. Do you think historical inaccuracy is relatively unimportant because it's only the Bible's spiritual content that matters?
3. In this book, God first uses dreams and visions and then a hand to reveal important things - how does he reveal things to us today?
4. Are there areas of your life where the "weighing" of friends, family and peers could become more important than God's?
5. Should the fact that "God holds in his hand your life" (see Daniel 4:23) comfort or concern you – why?
6. Is God's 'handwriting at the cross' intelligible to you? Could you use this illustration to enlighten others with God's help?

CHAPTER SIX: FACED WITH INJUSTICE

At the time of writing, the famous United States basketballer, Michael Jordan, has just been featured in the news, commenting on the number of black people shot by police in the US, and the revenge killings of police officers by blacks – all of which had been trending in news bulletins. He went on record as saying: "As a proud American, a father who lost his own dad in a senseless act of violence, and a black man, I have been deeply troubled by the deaths of African-Americans at the hands of law enforcement and angered by the cowardly and hateful targeting and killing of police officers," Jordan said in a statement. "I grieve with the families who have lost loved ones, as I know their pain all too well."

The concern there is about prejudice. The claim is that in some places people are stopped, searched and otherwise harassed for no other reason than the colour of their skin. In this chapter, the sixth from the book of Daniel, we find Daniel the victim of prejudice. "It seemed good to Darius to appoint 120 satraps over the kingdom, that they would be in charge of the whole kingdom, and over them three commissioners (of whom Daniel was one), that these satraps might be accountable to them, and that the king might not suffer loss. Then this Daniel began distinguishing himself among the commissioners and satraps because he possessed an extraordinary spirit, and the king planned to appoint him over the entire kingdom. Then the commissioners and satraps began trying to find a ground of accusation against Daniel in regard to government affairs; but they could find no ground of accusation or evidence of corruption, inasmuch as he was faithful, and no negligence or corruption was to be found in him.

Then these men said, "We will not find any ground of accusation against this Daniel unless we find it against him with regard to the law of his God." Then these commissioners and satraps came by agreement to the king and spoke to him as follows: "King Darius, live forever! "All the commissioners of the kingdom, the prefects and the satraps, the high officials and the governors have consulted together that the king should establish a statute and enforce an injunction that anyone who makes a petition to any god or man besides you, O king, for thirty days, shall be cast into the lions' den. Now, O king, establish the injunction and sign the document so that it may not be changed, according to the law of the Medes and Persians, which may not be revoked." Therefore King Darius signed the document, that is, the injunction. Now when Daniel knew that the document was signed, he entered his house (now in his roof chamber he had windows open toward Jerusalem); and he continued kneeling on his knees three times a day, praying and giving thanks before his God, as he had been doing previously.

Then these men came by agreement and found Daniel making petition and supplication before his God. Then they approached and spoke before the king about the king's injunction, "Did you not sign an injunction that any man who makes a petition to any god or man besides you, O king, for thirty days, is to be cast into the lions' den?" The king replied, "The statement is true, according to the law of the Medes and Persians, which may not be revoked." Then they answered and spoke before the king, "Daniel, who is one of the exiles from Judah, pays no attention to you, O king, or to the injunction which you signed, but keeps making his petition three times a day" (Daniel 6:1-13).

That's an example of someone on the receiving end of prejudice. There's no reason given for why those other officials wanted rid of Daniel. Sure, they were jealous. They'd have loved the extra promotion he was lined up for. But to go to these lengths, and have their rival condemned to death? It certainly didn't help that Daniel was a foreigner with other beliefs. From our earliest days, we remember in the school playground how cruel young children could be to anyone who was different. Often they were the object of aggressive bullying – and it would just come down to the fact that in some way they were different, either in how they looked, or spoke or even in how they moved due to perhaps some kind of disability. It was cruel, and it was ugly, unreasonable prejudice. It's the same here with Daniel.

He was also the butt of injustice. That's also been in the news in the United Kingdom. One large sportswear retailer has been criticized for treating its employees unfairly: with low pay, harsh conditions and with severe penalties being applied for trivial offences such as being one minute late for work. Have you ever been subjected to unfair treatment? Then you know what it feels like. It makes you want to shout out against it; to cry for justice; to try to get something done about it and get it all sorted.

Daniel was equally someone here in chapter 6 of his book who was subjected to injustice. The plot against him was clearly unfair. Daniel didn't deserve to be treated like that. The fact that his jealous colleagues who were prejudiced against him could find no legitimate cause of complaint against Daniel proves the total injustice Daniel was facing. Now, here's a question. Daniel's God was the God of heaven, why then did God do nothing about his servant's plight? We know God was pleased with Daniel's life. We're told repeatedly that God delighted in him and even desired his happiness. So why then is heaven silent in the face of the massive and blatant injustice Daniel is experiencing at the hands of these men?

Isn't that a question we're often asked? Not about Daniel, but about any contemporary injustice in the world. 'Huh,' many people scoff, 'there can't be a fair God – at least not one who's got any power at all – else why does he allow this to happen?' Many use this idea as an excuse not to believe in God's existence, or at least to profess not to believe.

Well, that sort of brings up the topic of religion, doesn't it? Those men who made plans against Daniel, who plotted his downfall, were cynically prepared to use his religion against him for their political ends. We see this kind of thing today, too. I remember the story of a nurse on a home visit (in the UK). After she had attended very professionally and caringly upon her patient, she requested permission that she might pray for her. This was declined, but the nurse was also reported and suspended from duty. Then again, symbols of one religion are at times permitted to be worn in public in the workplace, but not symbols of another religion. The way in which religion gets bandied about is all very political, and more and more expressions of faith are squeezed out of the public sphere. It's worse still when laws are passed which flatly contradict God's commands. But back to Daniel, and the deafening silence from heaven, as inexplicably God permits the abuse of his servant. So, what happened to Daniel?

"Then, as soon as the king heard this statement, he was deeply distressed and set his mind on delivering Daniel; and even until sunset he kept exerting himself to rescue him. Then these men came by agreement to the king and said to the king, "Recognize, O king, that it is a law of the Medes and Persians that no injunction or statute which the king establishes may be changed." Then the king gave orders, and Daniel was brought in and cast into the lions' den. The king spoke and said to Daniel, "Your God whom you constantly serve will Himself deliver you." A stone was brought and laid over the mouth of the den; and the king sealed it with his own signet ring and with the signet rings of his nobles, so that nothing would be changed in regard to Daniel.

Then the king went off to his palace and spent the night fasting, and no entertainment was brought before him; and his sleep fled from him. Then the king arose at dawn, at the break of day, and went in haste to the lions' den. When he had come near the den to Daniel, he cried out with a troubled voice. The king spoke and said to Daniel, "Daniel, servant of the living God, has your God, whom you constantly serve, been able to deliver you from the lions?" Then Daniel spoke to the king, "O king, live forever! "My God sent His angel and shut the lions' mouths and they have not harmed me, inasmuch as I was found innocent before Him; and also toward you, O king, I have committed no crime."

Then the king was very pleased and gave orders for Daniel to be taken up out of the den. So Daniel was taken up out of the den and no injury whatever was found on him, because he had trusted in his God. Then Darius the king wrote to all the peoples, nations and men of every language who were living in all the land: "May your peace abound! I make a decree that in all the dominion of my kingdom men are to fear and tremble before the God of Daniel; for He is the living God and enduring forever, and His kingdom is one which will not be destroyed, and His dominion will be forever" (Daniel 6:14-26).

I want you to notice with me how there had been no protest from the victim before his accusers nor before the king, as he was being led away to the lions. Daniel speaks out only after the stone is rolled away to reveal that God has vindicated him. And that ending to the incident we've just read shows how God was ultimately glorified in the delivery of the godly from trial.

As we've thought, in a world of prejudice and injustice, where religion is politicized and legislation contravenes God's decrees, God's silence is baffling to many, as is his allowing the abuse of his faithful followers. But, from the far side of the stone that was rolled away when Jesus defeated death, his New Testament spokespersons proclaim ultimate justice is coming. They tell of a day in which God will judge this world through Jesus Christ who died and rose again (Acts 17:31). Then ultimate justice will be served, and every wrong set to right, and all will glorify God for the fact that he knew when to be silent and when to speak, and how to vindicate the righteous at the right time so that in the end his name is glorified.

CHAPTER SIX STUDY QUESTIONS

1. Have you ever felt that you'd been treated unfairly – did you respond like Daniel?
2. What conclusion did you come to as to why God allowed it to happen?
3. How could you develop the material in this chapter into an apologetic-type of defence of why a loving God patiently permits unjust suffering in this world?
4. How does Daniel's treatment and response remind you of Jesus (see Isaiah 53:7-12)?
5. The prohibition on prayer was only for 30 days – couldn't Daniel simply have 'taken a break' or prayed in secret and defused the situation? How might we be tempted to compromise under pressure as Christians today?
6. Daniel's enemies were certain they would immediately catch him 'red-handed' in prayer, and they did – what kind of reputation precedes us?

CHAPTER SEVEN: THE RISE AND FALL OF WORLD EMPIRES

I have books on my bookshelves in a few different languages but, apart from an 'interlinear' Bible, each book is consistently in one particular language. The book of Daniel, however, was written in Hebrew except for the section from chapter 2 (from verse 4) through chapter 7 which was written in the more international Aramaic language. Interestingly, this is the section of Daniel's writing which shares with us God's international program for this world. It's a program which starts in the 6th century BC.

As we learn history at school we're taught certain dates, such as 1492 when Columbus sailed to discover the so-called New World of the Americas. But there's one date you won't typically learn in school despite the fact that it's one of the most important dates in world history. It's found in Jeremiah 25:1. It's there we read about "the first year of Nebuchadnezzar king of Babylon." He's, of course, the same character as we read about in the book of Daniel. The time of Nebuchadnezzar marked the beginning of "the times of the Gentiles" (Luke 21:24). This was a time when God judged his favoured people, Israel, and granted that world sovereignty should pass into Gentile hands. More details are now given to Daniel in chapter 7 through a dream:

"In the first year of Belshazzar king of Babylon Daniel saw a dream and visions in his mind as he lay on his bed; then he wrote the dream down and related the following summary of it. Daniel said, 'I was looking in my vision by night, and behold, the four winds of heaven were stirring up the great sea. And four great beasts were coming up from the sea, different from one another.

The first was like a lion and had the wings of an eagle. I kept looking until its wings were plucked, and it was lifted up from the ground and made to stand on two feet like a man; a human mind also was given to it. And behold, another beast, a second one, resembling a bear. And it was raised up on one side, and three ribs were in its mouth between its teeth; and thus they said to it, 'Arise, devour much meat!'

After this I kept looking, and behold, another one, like a leopard, which had on its back four wings of a bird; the beast also had four heads, and dominion was given to it. After this I kept looking in the night visions, and behold, a fourth beast, dreadful and terrifying and extremely strong; and it had large iron teeth. It devoured and crushed and trampled down the remainder with its feet; and it was different from all the beasts that were before it, and it had ten horns.

While I was contemplating the horns, behold, another horn, a little one, came up among them, and three of the first horns were pulled out by the roots before it; and behold, this horn possessed eyes like the eyes of a man and a mouth uttering great boasts. I kept looking until thrones were set up, and the Ancient of Days took His seat; His vesture was like white snow and the hair of His head like pure wool. His throne was ablaze with flames, its wheels were a burning fire. A river of fire was flowing and coming out from before Him; thousands upon thousands were attending Him, and myriads upon myriads were standing before Him; the court sat, and the books were opened.

Then I kept looking because of the sound of the boastful words which the horn was speaking; I kept looking until the beast was slain, and its body was destroyed and given to the burning fire. As for the rest of the beasts, their dominion was taken away, but an extension of life was granted to them for an appointed period of time. I kept looking in the night visions, and behold, with the clouds of heaven One like a Son of Man was coming, and He came up to the Ancient of Days and was presented before Him. And to Him was given dominion, glory and a kingdom, that all the peoples, nations and men of every language might serve Him. His dominion is an everlasting dominion which will not pass away; and His kingdom is one which will not be destroyed.

As for me, Daniel, my spirit was distressed within me, and the visions in my mind kept alarming me. I approached one of those who were standing by and began asking him the exact meaning of all this. So he told me and made known to me the interpretation of these things: 'These great beasts, which are four in number, are four kings who will arise from the earth. But the saints of the Highest One will receive the kingdom and possess the kingdom forever, for all ages to come'" (Daniel 7:1-18).

This dream given to Daniel is another version of the dream Daniel has previously interpreted for Nebuchadnezzar in chapter 2. You may recall he'd seen a huge statue portrayed in four metals: a head of gold; chest of silver; thighs of bronze and legs of iron – with feet of part iron and part clay. In each case, we've heard the stated interpretation. The four metals, and likewise now the four beasts, represented four successive world empires which would rule the earth. We've no need to speculate about the identity of the first three. I'll leave you to check it out from comparing surrounding verses in chapters 2 and 8 (Daniel 2:38; 8:20-21) that the first three of the empires are identified in the text of Scripture as the Babylonian, the Medo-Persian and the Greek empires.

You'll now recall that we've already presented compelling archaeological evidence to support that this book of Daniel was written at the time of the Babylonian empire in the 6th century BC. So, what's now familiar to us from history was at this time an amazing prophetic vision of coming empires the world had not yet heard of. Nor are these merely vague ramblings capable of various, very flexible and generous interpretations, they are pin-sharp in their details, even permitting us to identify historical characters such as Alexander the Great in the pages of our Bibles – except, remember, it was written some 200 years before he came on the scene!

Okay, so it's thrilling to have such confirmation that in the Bible we're not only dealing with the most accurate historical document, but we also have evidence of its divine origin. But the Babylonians, the Medo-Persian and Greek empires, well that's all water under the bridge now, what about things yet to befall this planet? Over to Daniel again:

"Then I desired to know the exact meaning of the fourth beast, which was different from all the others, exceedingly dreadful, with its teeth of iron and its claws of bronze, and which devoured, crushed and trampled down the remainder with its feet, and the meaning of the ten horns that were on its head and the other horn which came up, and before which three of them fell, namely, that horn which had eyes and a mouth uttering great boasts and which was larger in appearance than its associates. I kept looking, and that horn was waging war with the saints and overpowering them until the Ancient of Days came and judgment was passed in favor of the saints of the Highest One, and the time arrived when the saints took possession of the kingdom.

Thus he said: 'The fourth beast will be a fourth kingdom on the earth, which will be different from all the other kingdoms and will devour the whole earth and tread it down and crush it. As for the ten horns, out of this kingdom ten kings will arise; and another will arise after them, and he will be different from the previous ones and will subdue three kings. He will speak out against the Most High and wear down the saints of the Highest One, and he will intend to make alterations in times and in law; and they will be given into his hand for a time, times, and half a time. But the court will sit for judgment, and his dominion will be taken away, annihilated and destroyed forever. Then the sovereignty, the dominion and the greatness of all the kingdoms under the whole heaven will be given to the people of the saints of the Highest One; His kingdom will be an everlasting kingdom, and all the dominions will serve and obey Him'" (Daniel 7:19-27).

The fourth world empire which is portrayed here in Daniel chapter 7 as a most dreadful beast, one which almost defied description, corresponds with the fourth metal section of the image or statue seen by Nebuchadnezzar as interpreted by Daniel in chapter 2. There we read about the statue having legs of iron and feet partly of iron and partly of clay. This would be an utterly crushing empire, albeit one that would be characterised by internal division. Both visions make it clear that this refers to an empire which followed on in historical sequence from the Greek Empire but which will again be in existence when the Lord Jesus Christ returns to this earth to take up his power and rule on earth for a thousand years (as foretold in Revelation 20:1-10).

In contrast to the previous three world empires which are explicitly interpreted for us in the Bible, this fourth one is not named, and so we have to attempt cautiously to supply the interpretation. I say cautiously because the Apostle Peter reminds us (in 2 Peter 1:19) that using the prophetic Scriptures is like seeing our way by lamplight; whereas when events in time fulfil the predictions then suddenly everything becomes as clear as in bright daylight. This is how it happened with Christ's first Advent (coming), and it'll be no different with his second.

Many Bible students have for a long time favoured the view that the fourth empire is the Roman Empire. The two legs of Daniel statue are thought to represent the western and eastern divisions of the empire. Daniel chapter 9 describes the people who destroyed Jerusalem in AD 70 as people ethnically associated with the coming final world leader, also known as 'the antichrist.' The book of Revelation uses symbolism which is suggestive of the Roman Empire, especially in its religious form. Those Bible students became excited with the signing of 'the Treaty of Rome' in 1958 and have watched closely developments towards some kind of federated superstate across European lands very roughly re-occupying the territory Rome once held sway over. Their eyes are on Europe and a future European strongman who'll dominate the nations. That may not be far from the mark, but another contender is emerging which merits consideration.

All the other empires Daniel writes about were centred geographically on Babylon, even if it was no longer their principal city. The Roman Empire's boundary was always way to the west of Babylon, but there has been another historic empire which was centred territorially around Babylon, an empire in character far more crushing than Rome. What's more, it's been more fundamentally marked by division almost from its beginning: a division into Sunni and Shia factions. It, too, existed for many centuries and was not abolished until 1924 by Ataturk. We are now living in turbulent times when it is in the process of being re-established. Keep your eyes on the prophecies of Daniel!

CHAPTER SEVEN STUDY QUESTIONS

1. What appears to be the significance of God's program for the world internationally being shared in one language, while his program for Israel was shared in another?
2. Why do you think God, in effect, repeated the vision of the four world empires?
3. In what way is the fourth beast different from the first three (see Daniel 7:7,10)?
4. Who are the "saints of the Most High" in Daniel 7:25?
5. What is your understanding of verses 13 & 14? How does Daniel depict the end of the fourth kingdom?
6. How is the kingdom of the Most High different from the four world empires?

CHAPTER EIGHT: THE BRILLIANT MADMAN WHO HATED ISRAEL

We've previously seen that chapter 7 of Daniel contains much that's relevant for today and the time still to come. By contrast, chapter 8 gives us more detail of a section of the same prophecy which has by now been fulfilled historically. Horns, taken as symbols of power, are common to both chapters where they represent powerful human leaders who dominate the earth. But there's a difference which, if not observed, causes confusion. The principal 'horn' in chapter 7 is associated with the end-time of the fourth empire, and so points to the antichrist. However, in chapter 8 which we now come to, the notable 'horn' is identified with the third empire and is a detailed pen portrait of a notorious historical character of the 2nd century BC. His actions, however, serve as a sinister foreshadowing of the even more malevolent conduct of a future world leader, known as the antichrist. This is especially so when we consider his treatment of the state of Israel. Well, let's take a look with Daniel at his follow-up vision:

"In the third year of the reign of Belshazzar the king a vision appeared to me, Daniel, subsequent to the one which appeared to me previously. I looked in the vision, and while I was looking I was in the citadel of Susa, which is in the province of Elam; and I looked in the vision and I myself was beside the Ulai Canal. Then I lifted my eyes and looked, and behold, a ram which had two horns was standing in front of the canal. Now the two horns were long, but one was longer than the other, with the longer one coming up last. I saw the ram butting westward, northward, and southward, and no other beasts could stand before him nor was there anyone to rescue from his power, but he did as he pleased and magnified himself" (Daniel 8:1-4).

If I may just interject and help us along here. What I'm now going to say will be confirmed later in the text itself, but you should at this point understand that the two-horned ram represents the Medo-Persian empire. The Medes and the Persians were never equal partners, and so we have horns of different length. The Persians rose to power later and overshadowed the Medes. Now, wait a moment, for here come the Greeks!

"While I was observing [*Daniel says*], behold, a male goat was coming from the west over the surface of the whole earth without touching the ground; and the goat had a conspicuous horn between his eyes [*Well, that horn will be Alexander the Great of history*]. He came up to the ram that had the two horns, which I had seen standing in front of the canal, and rushed at him in his mighty wrath. I saw him come beside the ram, and he was enraged at him; and he struck the ram and shattered his two horns, and the ram had no strength to withstand him. So he hurled him to the ground and trampled on him, and there was none to rescue the ram from his power. Then the male goat magnified himself exceedingly. But as soon as he was mighty, the large horn was broken; and in its place there came up four conspicuous horns toward the four winds of heaven" (Daniel 8:5-8).

We're told later about the effect of the vision on Daniel, but what about its effect on you? There's probably a little confusion, so let's try to help unpack it. Alexander the Great (the prominent horn, see Daniel 8:5) came from the west with a small but fast army. He was enraged (v.6) at the Persians for having defeated the Greeks at the Battle of Marathon (490 BC) and the Battle of Salamis (481 BC), these being Greek cities near Athens. He quickly conquered Asia Minor, Syria, Egypt, and Mesopotamia in a few years, beginning in 334 BC. The Persians were helpless to resist him (v.7), but then Alexander died of malaria and the effects of alcoholism in 323 BC at the age of 32 in Babylon. 'As soon as he was mighty,' and so unexpectedly prematurely, he was 'broken' (v.8).

Alexander had no son to succeed him, so his empire was split among his four generals, represented here by the four horns (compare v.8; see Daniel 11:4). Two of those generals are of particular interest to us. They are Ptolemy and Seleucus. Egypt was given to Ptolemy; while Syria was given to Seleucus. Now let's return to the words spoken to Daniel concerning those four generals who followed on from Alexander the Great:

"Out of one of them *[that is, out of one of the four horns representing the four generals who succeeded Alexander]* came forth a rather small horn which grew exceedingly great toward the south, toward the east, and toward the Beautiful Land. It grew up to the host of heaven and caused some of the host and some of the stars to fall to the earth, and it trampled them down. It even magnified itself to be equal with the Commander of the host; and it removed the regular sacrifice from Him, and the place of His sanctuary was thrown down. And on account of transgression the host will be given over to the horn along with the regular sacrifice; and it will fling truth to the ground and perform its will and prosper" (Daniel 8:9-12).

Daniel is then given help in understanding the vision, for which we, too, are grateful. It begins with a little recap which I hope will also be useful to us: "The ram which you saw with the two horns represents the kings of Media and Persia. The shaggy goat represents the kingdom of Greece, and the large horn that is between his eyes is the first king. The broken horn and the four horns that arose in its place represent four kingdoms which will arise from his nation, although not with his power. In the latter period of their rule, When the transgressors have run their course, a king will arise, insolent and skilled in intrigue. His power will be mighty, but not by his own power, and he will destroy to an extraordinary degree and prosper and perform his will; He will destroy mighty men and the holy people. And through his shrewdness He will cause deceit to succeed by his influence; and he will magnify himself in his heart, and he will destroy many while they are at ease. He will even oppose the Prince of princes, but he will be broken without human agency" (Daniel 8:20-25).

From among the four horns, that is the four generals, there would arise, Gabriel said, a severe and cunning king. He'd be a powerful ruler who would devastate property and destroy people in order to expand his kingdom. The holy people, the nation of Israel ('saints,' Daniel 7:18,22,27), would be his special target. His rise to power was not to be his own doing (Daniel 8:24) and equally his downfall was not by human means (this particular man, whom we'll identity shortly, died insane in Persia in 163 BC).

What we're now seeing is that this part of the vision anticipated the rise of a ruler originating from within the Greek Empire who had come to subjugate Israel, desecrate her temple, interrupt her worship, and demand for himself the authority and worship that belongs only to God.

The ruler being referred to here is known to history as Antiochus IV Epiphanes. After murdering his brother, who'd inherited the throne in the Seleucid dynasty, he came to power in 175 BC. Five years later, Ptolemy VI of Egypt tried to regain territory which was then ruled over by Antiochus. In response, Antiochus invaded Egypt and defeated Ptolemy VI and even proclaimed himself king in Egypt. This was his growth in power 'toward the south' (v.9). On his return from this conquest, trouble broke out in Jerusalem so he decided to subdue Jerusalem ('the Beautiful Land,' v.9). The people were subjugated, the temple desecrated, and the temple treasury plundered.

From this conquest Antiochus returned to Egypt in 168 BC, but was forced out by Rome. On his return, he decided he'd make the land of Israel a buffer zone between himself and Egypt. So, he attacked and burned Jerusalem, killing lots of people (see Daniel 8:10). The Jews were forbidden to keep the Sabbath, their annual feasts, and their traditional sacrifices. Altars to idols were set up in Jerusalem and on December 16, 167 BC, the Jews were ordered to offer unclean sacrifices and to eat swine's flesh or else be put to death. For how long would this harsh treatment of the Jews be permitted, you may be wondering? Daniel chapter 8 again supplies the answer:

"Then I heard a holy one speaking, and another holy one said to that particular one who was speaking, 'How long will the vision about the regular sacrifice apply, while the transgression causes horror, so as to allow both the holy place and the host to be trampled?' He said to me, 'For 2,300 evenings and mornings; then the holy place will be properly restored'" (Daniel 8:13-14).

That reference to "evenings and mornings" may be to the daily evening and morning sacrifices in Israel (Numbers 28:4), which were interrupted by Antiochus' desecration. With two sacrifices made daily, the 2,300 offerings would cover just over three years (of 360 days each) – which is the time from Antiochus' desecration of the temple (December 16, 167 BC) to the refurbishing and restoring of the temple by Judas Maccabeus in late 164 BC and on into 163 BC when all the Jewish sacrifices were fully restored.

So, what we've seen is that Daniel chapter 8 reveals Israel's history under the Seleucids and particularly under Antiochus during the time of Greek domination. But it also points forward to give an indication of what will be Israel's experiences under the Antichrist, whom Antiochus foreshadows. From Antiochus we can learn more about the coming desecrator: He'll achieve great power by subduing others (v.24). He'll rise to power by promising false security (v.25). He'll be intelligent and persuasive (v.23). He'll be controlled by another (v.24), that is, Satan. He'll be an adversary of Israel and subjugate Israel to his authority (vv.24-25). He'll rise up in opposition to the Prince of princes, the Lord Jesus Christ (v.25). And his rule will be brought to an end by divine intervention (v.25). If you're a believer on the Lord Jesus Christ, you'll be glad to know that he'll come to take us away before this coming time of distress for Israel (Jeremiah 30:7).

CHAPTER EIGHT STUDY QUESTIONS

1. What's the reason for this 'horn' being different from the 'horn' in the previous chapter?
2. Are there any detailed features of the vision which impress you with their accuracy?
3. Can you discover why a year was deemed to be 360 days in length and not 365?
4. Do you agree with the explanation given of the 2,300 evenings and mornings? If not, why not?
5. How can we be confident that believers will not experience the time of the Antichrist?

CHAPTER NINE: DANIEL'S SEVENTY 'SEVENS'

After straddling an overnight change of world empire (in chapter 5), and facing a den full of once slavering lions (in chapter 6), and then absorbing the most appalling apocalyptic visions (of chapter 7), Daniel has probably by now entered the role of being an elder statesman. And so we arrive now at the beginning of Daniel chapter 9:

"In the first year of Darius the son of Ahasuerus, of Median descent, who was made king over the kingdom of the Chaldeans - in the first year of his reign, I, Daniel, observed in the books the number of the years which was revealed as the word of the LORD to Jeremiah the prophet for the completion of the desolations of Jerusalem, namely, seventy years. So I gave my attention to the Lord God to seek Him by prayer and supplications, with fasting, sackcloth and ashes" (Daniel 9:1-3).

So, Daniel has one day, in his daily devotions, opened the Bible book of Jeremiah the prophet and he's 'arrested' – not by people spying on him in secret this time, but by the Spirit of God – for Daniel has just discovered that in God's prescribed will, the discipline of his people - even their banishment away from Jerusalem - would be for a 70-year term. What excites him is that he now realizes that the time is up! He turns this fresh information into passionate prayer. Daniel, the 'man of desirability' in God's eyes, having been stopped in his tracks when reading his Bible, now turns his Bible-reading into what seems like a breathless, staccato prayer.

"I prayed to the LORD my God and confessed and said, "Alas, O Lord, the great and awesome God, who keeps His covenant and lovingkindness for those who love Him and keep His commandments, we have sinned, committed iniquity, acted wickedly and rebelled, even turning aside from Your commandments and ordinances. O Lord, in accordance with all Your righteous acts, let now Your anger and Your wrath turn away from Your city Jerusalem, Your holy mountain; for because of our sins and the iniquities of our fathers, Jerusalem and Your people have become a reproach to all those around us. So now, our God, listen to the prayer of Your servant and to his supplications, and for Your sake, O Lord, let Your face shine on Your desolate sanctuary" (Daniel 9:4-5, 16-17).

Your 'desolate sanctuary,' he says. It had been 50 years since a temple last stood at Jerusalem, and 70 years since the deportation of God's people began, and many more than that since Daniel's compatriots had first begun to spurn God's laws. But I want to show you that though the Babylonians may have succeeded in taking the man of God away from the house of God, the Babylonians and Persians had spectacularly failed to take God's house away from God's man.

What do I mean by that? Allow me to explain. Daniel's daily schedule of time-keeping is still being regulated by the timetable of the altar belonging to God's house at Jerusalem – the one which by this time had been demolished at least 50 years before. What's even more revealing is the fact that his undistracted thoughts are overshadowed by the spectre of the desolate sanctuary. And his outlook is ever through the open window of his prayer chamber, a window strategically opened toward the place of God's Name at Jerusalem. Let me show you where I'm getting all that from because it has again made such an impression on me that I really want to share it with you. First, we read that Daniel "went to his house where he had windows in his upper chamber open toward Jerusalem (Daniel 6:10) and in Daniel chapter 9 we hear him praying:

"'O Lord, hear; O Lord, forgive. O Lord, pay attention and act. Delay not, for your own sake, O my God, because your city and your people are called by your name.' While I was speaking and praying, confessing my sin and the sin of my people Israel, and presenting my plea before the LORD my God for the holy hill of my God, while I was speaking in prayer, the man Gabriel, whom I had seen in the vision at the first, came to me in swift flight at the time of the evening sacrifice" (Daniel 9:19-21).

By way of application, may I ask: If it were you in a minority of one against the world, do you think you would retain your convictions about God and his house and what it means to be in a New Testament Church of God? Finally, let's now consider what Gabriel went on to tell Daniel. God has shared with Daniel, in chapters 2 and 7, his plan for the Gentile world at large, in terms of the four great successive empires from the time of the 6th century BC right through until the time of Christ's return to earth to set up his kingdom. In chapter 9 of Daniel, God now shares with his servant his plan for Daniel's own people, the Jewish people. Gabriel now tells Daniel:

"Seventy weeks have been decreed for your people and your holy city, to finish the transgression, to make an end of sin, to make atonement for iniquity, to bring in everlasting righteousness, to seal up vision and prophecy and to anoint the most holy place. So you are to know and discern that from the issuing of a decree to restore and rebuild Jerusalem until Messiah the Prince there will be seven weeks and sixty-two weeks; it will be built again, with plaza and moat, even in times of distress. Then after the sixty-two weeks the Messiah will be cut off and have nothing, and the people of the prince who is to come will destroy the city and the sanctuary.

And its end will come with a flood; even to the end there will be war; desolations are determined. And he will make a firm covenant with the many for one week, but in the middle of the week he will put a stop to sacrifice and grain offering; and on the wing of abominations will come one who makes desolate, even until a complete destruction, one that is decreed, is poured out on the one who makes desolate" (Daniel 9:24-27).

Seventy 'weeks' are literally seventy 'sevens' where each 'seven' is a unit of seven years. So, this is a total of 70 times 7, or 490, prophetic years (each of 360 days, which equals 476 ordinary solar years). Sixty-nine of them (all but the last one) stretch from the restoration of the city by the completion of its wall by Nehemiah in 444 BC all the way to the cross of Christ in AD 33. We've no time to explain the precision of that timing, but check it out for yourself. At the cross, when God's people rejected their Messiah, it was as if God stopped the prophetic clock with one 'week,' or one final seven-year period, left to run.

Daniel's clock starts ticking again when a leader, who'll dominate the world, signs a seven-year deal to guarantee the security of Israel's borders: "... the people of the prince who is to come will destroy the city and the sanctuary ... and he will make a firm covenant with the many for one week" (so says Daniel 9:26-27). The mention there of 'people' is seemingly a reference to the Roman people under Titus who destroyed Jerusalem and its temple in AD 70. So, 'the prince who is to come' seems at first to be a Roman prince (or a latter-day Caesar), that is a mid-European leader.

Sure, the last emperor abdicated in AD 476 and then power passed to the Roman Catholic Church; its popes crowning many

Handwritten margin note (left side): 483 × 360/365·25 = 476

Handwritten margin note (left side, lower): 69 × 7 = 483

'Holy Roman Emperors.' The eastern empire continued much longer into the 15th century. The Club of Rome then formed in 1968 (allegedly with a blueprint for world government in ten regions). But we need to ask: 'How secure is this identification of Daniel's fourth kingdom with the Roman Empire?' What has led many to that conclusion? Well, in addition to the ethnicity of the people of the prince as mentioned, there are the two legs of the statue feasibly picturing the western and eastern division of the Roman Empire, together with allusions in the book of Revelation to the 'city which reigns' and the 'seven mountains' – often taken as pointing to the Roman city of the seven hills which was dominant in the time of the Apostle John. But there are other ways of looking at these things.

A closer investigation actually reveals something potentially very significant: the Roman soldiers under Titus' command in AD 70 were not Italians or Europeans. Tacitus tells us Titus found three legions in Judea, added one from Syria, and two from Alexandria – to which was added a strong contingent of Arabs. Josephus likewise agrees it was an army dominated by 'provincials.' The troops, then, were the ancestors of modern day inhabitants of the Middle East, mainly Arabs (Syrians and Turks) and NOT Europeans! Josephus adds: the ethnic legions were out of control, 'their passions too hard for the regards they had for Caesar ... thus was the holy house burnt down, without Caesar's approbation' (Wars of the Jews).

If then the Islamic Caliphate (IC or ISIS) can be considered a contender for Daniel's fourth world empire, with a rival claim to that of the Roman empire, then we pause to note that division has characterised Islam from Muhammad's time into 15% Shia (succession by relatives) and 85% Sunnis (succession by companions) – could these be the two legs of Daniel's image?

While the Islamic State ruled previously in history for thirteen hundred years, ending in 1924 with the secular Turkish reformer Ataturk, the Roman Empire's borders remained mostly 500 miles west of Babylon, which is somewhat awkward as Daniel's vision was otherwise a Babylon-centric vision. Moreover, the Islamic Caliphate was 'a crushing empire' as is the fourth empire's Biblical depiction. So, there are arguments which make this alternative speculation worth considering.

Turning to today and the revival before our eyes of the Islamic State or Caliphate, the shrewd leaders of ISIS have nowadays combined two of the most powerful ideas in Islam - the return of the Islamic Empire and the end of the world – and they've fused them into a mission and message that shapes its overall strategy and inspires its army of zealous and ruthless fighters. All of which might mean that the gruesome imagery of Revelation chapter 17, where we see a woman astride a fearsome beast, represents a literally Babylon-centric Islam controlling a Mid-eastern Muslim Empire whose reign of terror will be felt even across Europe.

Or maybe it's a hybrid picture implicating apostate Christendom and involving Europe directly: so-called Chrislam influencing Eurabia. The Islamic State with its preferred mode of execution being beheading and its crescent moon symbolism fits well with what we read of in the Bible's last apocalyptic book of Revelation which largely focuses on what will happen on earth during Daniel's 70th 'seven' – the one that's still future. World religion appears to be heading back to its roots in a Babylonian-style moon-god religion (see Revelation 17 and Genesis 10).

CHAPTER NINE STUDY QUESTIONS

1. Can you recall a time when you made a discovery through reading your Bible that really excited and energized you?
2. Daniel turned his Bible study into prayer. Is this a helpful model to inform our prayer times? Please qualify your answer.
3. Daniel had a practice of praying at set times in front of his open window, facing Jerusalem – what other practices could you adopt in your prayer times that might help you?
4. Try to check out how the 69 'weeks' starting at 444 BC give a precise prediction which confirms the best scientific evidence for the date of the crucifixion in 33 AD.
5. The number 7 appears frequently in these chapters – what do scholars believe is the significance of the number in the Bible?

CHAPTER TEN: SPIRITUAL WARFARE

Are you cynical about answered prayer? Well, take a grandstand seat as we come now to the tenth chapter of the book of Daniel, and just watch what happens when you take a man of godly integrity, someone who's correctly understanding God's agenda from the Bible and above all who means business with God in fired-up prayer. It's here we'll find the workings of prayer being exposed for us.

It's Daniel, of course, whose prayer penetrates heaven and who's the one who's instrumental in getting God's house back in operation far away at Jerusalem. Would you not agree that this is the greatest accomplishment of Daniel's life?

But how can we know all this? Well, at the beginning of chapter 10, in the third year of Cyrus, Daniel receives his final vision, the one which will be interpreted to him in chapter 11. So, this is at least a couple of years after the change of empire described at the end of chapter 5 with the fall of Babylon and Belshazzar. The Medes and Persians are power-sharing and they refer to their king(s) as Darius and Cyrus, respectively. By this time any of Daniel's people who had a desire to do so had been officially permitted to return to Jerusalem and rebuild the temple there – that's the temple which had been destroyed by the previous Babylonian empire.

Could we just pause and think about this? That was an amazing turn of events! Imagine a pagan king finding it in his heart to facilitate the work of God in Jerusalem! This could only have been God's doing – and it was. The first verse of chapter 11 refers back to that time of empire change we've mentioned and gives us a wonderful insight into the mechanics of what actually happened. Remember, this would take us back to the time Daniel had been reading Jeremiah the prophet's writings and God revealed to him through his Bible reading that with the end of the Babylonian empire came the moment in God's plan for the return of Daniel's people to rebuild for God at Jerusalem (compare Daniel 11:1 with Daniel 9:1). Daniel then pours out an absolute model prayer of confession and intercession which is recorded for us in Daniel chapter 9.

That prayer penetrated heaven, and became decisive (so Daniel 11:1 informs us) in tipping the scales in a cosmic contest fought between angelic beings. Here's what Daniel's mysterious visitor says in Daniel 11:1: "In the first year of Darius the Mede, I arose to be an encouragement and a protection for him." Let me check - do you recall what we learn from Ephesians chapter 6? "For our struggle is not against flesh and blood, but against the rulers, against the powers, against the world forces of this darkness, against the spiritual forces of wickedness in the heavenly places. Therefore, take up the full armor of God ... With all prayer and petition pray at all times in the Spirit."

Is prayer sometimes a struggle for you? That's the way it should be! Prayer is a struggle in an unseen battleground. A lot happens when we pray which we can't imagine, but something of it is revealed in the case of Daniel's prayer. And what is shared here in Daniel aligns itself with the Apostle Paul's Ephesian commentary on our prayer struggle. Prayer engages in a cosmic conflict with unseen forces. So, armed with that biblical information, we come back to Daniel. Not only did Daniel's prayer penetrate heaven, and engage in an angelic contest, but the outcome was then projected down to earth. What are the words of a hymn we sometimes sing? 'Prayer moves the hand that moves the world to bring deliverance down.' That's exactly what happens here. The beginning of Daniel chapter 11 explains the outworking and powerful effect of Daniel's prayer from the beginning of chapter 9. His prayer engaged with the contest being waged in heaven against spiritual forces of wickedness.

Like a battle of minds being played out in manoeuvres on a chessboard, the ebb and flow in heavenly angelic warfare was played out at that time on earth in the fall and rise of world empires. Daniel's prayer, and the assistance of angels connected with it, brought about a strengthening of the position of Darius the Mede who was the one to take over the empire from Belshazzar. This was then soon afterwards reflected in the astounding foreign policy developments of the new empire – the ones we've talked about which led to God's temple being rebuilt.

It's absolutely breathtaking stuff. Really exciting reading. A wonderful encouragement to real praying. God's house is now back in operation far away at Jerusalem. This is the greatest accomplishment of Daniel's life, brought about through his Bible-reading and prayer time far away from the scene of the action.

Even if you're not as enthralled as I am by the prophecies of Daniel and intrigued by how they probably relate to what we're seeing happening today in the world around us, do take this away from our present study that the prayer of a righteous person - in tune with God's will revealed through his Word, the Bible, as he or she earnestly lays hold on God – achieves far more than we can imagine. Don't say that due to your confined circumstances 'all I can do is pray' – for that's the vital, and perhaps sometimes the missing, piece for the realization of God's plans and what he desires to take place on earth.

But, so far, we've hardly said anything about chapter 10 at all. We must remedy that now. We're told that in the third year of Cyrus (536 BC) a message was revealed to Daniel. It was true and he understood it (v.1). It also made a huge impact on Daniel. What had been communicated to Daniel – as we're going to see from its content in chapter 11 – was a forecast of protracted warfare involving Daniel's people, the people of Israel. If Daniel was overjoyed that some of his fellow-Jews were now back in Jerusalem on a temple re-building project (and I've no doubt he was) then this would come as a terrible shock to him. By means of the vision, he was allowed to peer down through the corridors of time, and he saw almost nothing but centuries of trouble ahead for his beloved nation and the city he himself had been torn away from in his youth. That's why he tells us:

"In those days, I, Daniel, had been mourning for three entire weeks. I did not eat any tasty food, nor did meat or wine enter my mouth, nor did I use any ointment at all until the entire three weeks were completed. On the twenty-fourth day of the first month, while I was by the bank of the great river, that is, the Tigris, I lifted my eyes and looked, and behold, there was a certain man dressed in linen, whose waist was girded with a belt of pure gold of Uphaz. His body also was like beryl, his face had the appearance of lightning, his eyes were like flaming torches, his arms and feet like the gleam of polished bronze, and the sound of his words like the sound of a tumult.

Then he said to me, 'Do not be afraid, Daniel, for from the first day that you set your heart on understanding this and on humbling yourself before your God, your words were heard, and I have come in response to your words. But the prince of the kingdom of Persia was withstanding me for twenty-one days; then behold, Michael, one of the chief princes, came to help me, for I had been left there with the kings of Persia. Now I have come to give you an understanding of what will happen to your people in the latter days, for the vision pertains to the days yet future'" (Daniel 10:2-6, 12-14).

Who was this interpreter of the vision? We're not told, so we can't be sure. Before now, the angel Gabriel has appeared to Daniel and spoken with him, but never with the kind of reaction from Daniel that's described here. Daniel was afraid, speechless, and left without strength at the awesome appearance of this visitor. Might this have been a pre-incarnate appearance of Israel's Messiah? His description leads me in that direction, but some consider it improbable that he should be delayed by an angelic prince. But do we, too, at times, not hinder God's working through us? Could this not be him speaking as the commander-in-chief of the armies of loyal angels – those who stood ready to help him in his human experience on earth?

Of course, there's no restraining of his power here by virtue of his having taken humanity yet, but does the Lord not exercise restraint such that his purpose is effected at the exact moment of his choice? In any case: "... he said [to Daniel], "Do you understand why I came to you? But I shall now return to fight against the prince of Persia; so I am going forth, and behold, the prince of Greece is about to come. However, I will tell you what is inscribed in the writing of truth. Yet there is no one who stands firmly with me against these forces except Michael your prince" (Daniel 10:20-21).

We return to the comment we made earlier concerning cosmic conflict: a warring between forces of good and evil in the spiritual dimension which has its physical counterpart in warfare between nations on this earth. Clearly, the named angel, Michael, has a special and prominent role as a guardian of the cause of God's ancient people, Israel.

Notice again the strategic part played by the prayer of God's biblically-informed servant who has a heart for God's glory. The one now standing before Daniel announces that he'd come in response to his prayer of three weeks earlier, and then graciously explains the delay by reference to how he'd been hindered for 21 days by the angelic prince of Persia. So, we learn to pray in God's will, as seen from Scripture, and to try not to be too impatient!

CHAPTER TEN STUDY QUESTIONS

1. Have there been times when you questioned the value of prayer? What led to that?
2. How has your perspective on prayer changed through studying Daniel chapter 10?
3. Who do you conclude Daniel's visitor was?
4. Is the condition and welfare of God's house today as big a priority for you as it was for Daniel?
5. Waiting for prayer to be answered can be difficult – what can help us?
6. Who would you consider to be the Bible's "prayer warriors" – what are their key attributes?

CHAPTER ELEVEN: THE BIBLE'S MOST DETAILED PROPHETIC CHAPTER

In this chapter, we hope to begin to look at what's perhaps the Bible's most detailed chapter. In terms of its sheer density of prophetic statements, it's remarkable. There are some 135 in the first 35 verses! To showcase just how impressive the inspired Word of God is, we're going to attempt to interweave the historical fulfilments in between the prophecies. It's the hallmark of deity that God can write up the future just easily as the past. The eleventh chapter begins:

"... Behold, three more kings are going to arise in Persia. Then a fourth will gain far more riches than all of them; as soon as he becomes strong through his riches, he will arouse the whole empire against the realm of Greece. And a mighty king will arise, and he will rule with great authority and do as he pleases. But as soon as he has arisen, his kingdom will be broken up and parceled out toward the four points of the compass, though not to his own descendants, nor according to his authority which he wielded, for his sovereignty will be uprooted and given to others besides them" (Daniel 11:2-4).

Daniel is informed that the present leadership in the Persian Empire would be succeeded by four rulers. History names them for us (Cambyses, Pseudo-Smerdis, Darius I Hystaspes, Xerxes). Xerxes, the fourth, was the most influential, and during his reign he fought wars against Greece. The 'mighty king' who would arise was Alexander the Great. Between 334 and 330 BC, he conquered Asia Minor, Syria, Egypt, and the land of the Medo-Persian Empire. A few years after his death, his kingdom was divided among his four generals: Seleucus (over Syria and Mesopotamia), Ptolemy (over Egypt), Lysimachus (over Thrace and portions of Asia Minor), and Cassander (over Macedonia and Greece).

The next section (vv.5-20) of this long eleventh chapter spotlights the conflict between the Ptolemies and the Seleucids. The Ptolemies who ruled over Egypt, were called 'the kings of the South.' The Seleucids, ruling over Syria, north of Israel, were called 'the kings of the North.' There follow many details of the pretty much continuous conflict between the Ptolemies and the Seleucids. During all this, the land of Israel was invaded first by one power and then by the other. Although we've no time to examine the details, every scriptural statement made in this section has had its precise fulfilment in history. In the first 35 verses of Daniel chapter 11, some 135 predictions were made which were all subsequently realized historically - so much so that skeptics insist on a later date for writing, but we've already seen how archaeology has established the author's contemporary knowledge of 6th century events which were unknown to later historians.

When we come to verse 21 of chapter eleven, a significant figure confronts us: "... a despicable person will arise, on whom the honor of kingship has not been conferred, but he will come in a time of tranquility and seize the kingdom by intrigue." Theses verses describe Antiochus IV Epiphanes. This one Seleucid king who ruled from 175 B.C. to 163 B.C. is given as much attention as all the others before him combined. This is not only because of his treatment of the land of Israel, but also because he foreshadows the antichrist who will one day soon again desecrate Israel's land.

Despite the throne rightly belonging to another, Antiochus IV Epiphanes seized it; so, he didn't become king by rightful succession, but through intrigue. Let's continue with our sort of prophetic/historic interlinear version of events: "The overflowing forces will be flooded away before him and shattered, and also the prince of the covenant" (Daniel 11:22).

He was accepted as ruler because he was able to turn aside an invading army, perhaps the Egyptians. He also deposed Onias III, the high priest, the prince of the covenant. "After an alliance is made with him he will practice deception, and he will go up and gain power with a small force of people. In a time of tranquility he will enter the richest parts of the realm, and he will accomplish what his fathers never did, nor his ancestors; he will distribute plunder, booty and possessions among them, and he will devise his schemes against strongholds, but only for a time" (Daniel 11:23-24).

After his military victories, Antiochus Epiphanes' prestige and power rose with the help of a comparatively small number of people. He evidently sought to bring peace to his realm by redistributing wealth, taking from the rich and giving to his followers.

"He will stir up his strength and courage against the king of the South with a large army; so the king of the South will mobilize an extremely large and mighty army for war; but he will not stand, for schemes will be devised against him. Those who eat his choice food will destroy him, and his army will overflow, but many will fall down slain. As for both kings, their hearts will be intent on evil, and they will speak lies to each other at the same table; but it will not succeed, for the end is still to come at the appointed time" (Daniel 11:25-27).

After Antiochus consolidated his kingdom, he moved against the Egyptian king of the South in 170 BC. In this battle the Egyptians had a large army but were defeated and Antiochus professed friendship with Egypt. The victor and the vanquished sat at a table together as though friendship had been established, but the goal of both to establish peace was never realized for they were both deceptive.

"Then he will return to his land with much plunder; but his heart will be set against the holy covenant, and he will take action and then return to his own land" (Daniel 11:28).

Antiochus carried great wealth back to his homeland from his conquest. On his return he passed through the land of Israel. He was frustrated because he'd wanted to take over all Egypt, so he took it out on the Jews by desecrating the Jerusalem temple, before returning to his own country.

"At the appointed time he will return and come into the South, but this last time it will not turn out the way it did before. For ships of Kittim will come against him; therefore he will be disheartened and will return and become enraged at the holy covenant and take action; so he will come back and show regard for those who forsake the holy covenant (Daniel 11:29-30).

Two years later (in 168 BC) Antiochus moved against Egypt again. As he did so, he was opposed by the Romans who'd come to Egypt in ships from the western coastlands (Kittim or Cyprus). This was a disheartening defeat for Antiochus Epiphanes, as he was left with no alternative but to return to his own land. For a second time Antiochus took out his frustration on the Jews, the city of Jerusalem, and their temple. He vented his fury against the law of Moses, and favoured any Jews who turned to help him. He desecrated the temple, abolishing the daily sacrifice. Antiochus sent his general and soldiers into Jerusalem on what was supposedly a peace mission. But they attacked on the Sabbath, killed many, and burned the city.

"Forces from him will arise, desecrate the sanctuary fortress, and do away with the regular sacrifice. And they will set up the abomination of desolation. By smooth words he will turn to godlessness those who act wickedly toward the covenant, but the people who know their God will display strength and take action. Those who have insight among the people will give understanding to the many; yet they will fall by sword and by flame, by captivity and by plunder for many days. Now when they fall they will be granted a little help, and many will join with them in hypocrisy. Some of those who have insight will fall, in order to refine, purge and make them pure until the end time; because it is still to come at the appointed time" (Daniel 11:31-35).

In trying to get rid of Judaism and enforce Greek culture on the Jews, Antiochus banned the Jews from following their religious practices and ordered copies of the Law to be burned. Then he set up the abomination of desolation. Worst of all, on December 16, 167 BC he built an altar to Zeus on the altar of burnt offering outside the Jewish temple, and offered a pig on it. Such desolations, as we saw, are again predicted at the close of the ninth chapter during the future time of the end-game of the Antichrist – something which the Lord Jesus spoke about in Matthew's Gospel, chapter 24.

Antiochus promised apostate Jews great reward if they would set aside their God and instead worship the god of Greece. Many were persuaded by his flattering promises and worshipped the false god. But a small remnant remained faithful. These were God-fearing people like Daniel's three companions, whom we've already used as illustrative examples of those who know God.

The Jews who refused to submit to Antiochus' false religious system were persecuted and martyred. In 166 BC, a man by the name of Mattathias refused to submit to this false religious system. He and his sons fled from Jerusalem to the mountains and began the Maccabean revolt. These times are remembered by Jews to this day in December every year at the feast of Hanukkah. At first only a few Jews joined the Maccabees. But as their movement became popular, many more joined. The suffering endured by the faithful served to refine and purify them. The persecution was of short duration, as had been previously revealed to Daniel in chapter 8. Here, in chapter 11, Daniel had been assured that this persecution would pass, for the section ends with a definite hint of things stretching far into the future, at God's appointed time. Surely this indicates the final days of the Antichrist, about whom we must speak in the next and final chapter (when we'll complete this eleventh chapter of Daniel) – hopefully with our confidence now riding high in the amazing accuracy of God's tried and tested Word!

CHAPTER ELEVEN STUDY QUESTIONS

1. What do you think is the importance of being able to identify notable historical figures, such as Alexander the Great in the Bible?
2. Beyond establishing historical authenticity, what else does this detailed chapter prove?
3. What support do you find here for the claim that some Bible prophecies have multiple fulfilments?
4. What is the 'holy covenant' referred to in v.28?

CHAPTER TWELVE: THE END

All the events described in Daniel chapter 11 until we get to verse 36 are now in the past – although some of them didn't take place until more than 300 years after Daniel had put down his 'pen.' All the mentioned intricate details of the conflicts between the kings of the north and south - between the Seleucids and the Ptolemies - were fulfilled exactly as Daniel had predicted. So exactly, in fact, that skeptics have denied that the book was written by Daniel in the 6th century BC, claiming it must have been written after the events took place, and during the time of the Maccabees (168 BC - 134 BC).

But God who knows the end of a thing from its beginning, can easily reveal the details of history in advance. Not only has he done that regarding events which we now regard as historical, but extending forwards from verse 36 we're going to see that he's also done the same for things which are still to happen. No critic can challenge these! And the outline of their realization would seem to be taking shape in the sensational events occurring today in the Middle East. Here's what verse 36 says: "Then the king will do as he pleases, and he will exalt and magnify himself above every god and will speak monstrous things against the God of gods; and he will prosper until the indignation is finished, for that which is decreed will be done."

"He will show no regard for the gods of his fathers or for the desire of women, nor will he show regard for any other god; for he will magnify himself above them all. But instead he will honor a god of fortresses, a god whom his fathers did not know; he will honor him with gold, silver, costly stones and treasures. He will take action against the strongest of fortresses with the help of a foreign god; he will give great honor to those who acknowledge him and will cause them to rule over the many, and will parcel out land for a price" (Daniel 11:37-39).

The events recorded in these verses will occur during the final seven years of the 70 'sevens' mentioned in Daniel 9:24; that is, they relate to the same future time and conditions on this earth which the book of Revelation (in chapters 6 through 18) describes. The book of Daniel is the key to unlocking the book of Revelation.

'The king who does as he pleases,' will take to himself absolute power in the religious realm, magnifying himself above all gods and defying and speaking blasphemously against the God of gods. His showing no regard for the gods of his fathers means that in order to gain absolute power in the religious realm, this king will have no respect for his religious heritage. He will at the very end set aside all organized religion, showing no regard for any god, and will set himself up as the sole object of worship. Instead of depending on gods, he'll depend on his own Satanic power, and by that power he'll demand all the world's worship. The fact he's no regard for the one desired by women probably suggests he despises the messianic hope of Israel. Many an Israelite woman had doubtless desired to become the mother of the coming Messiah.

The Antichrist will honor a god of fortresses, perhaps suggesting he'll promote military strength. And because of his political and religious power he'll be able to accumulate great wealth. The god unknown to his ancestors may refer to Satan. Although he comes to power by offering peace through a covenant with Israel (cf. Daniel 9:27), he's no stranger to military power – far from it.

So, what are the ultimate predictions for the last days based on Daniel 11? To a large extent it's a continuation of all that's gone before in the verses running up to verse 35. In other words, there will be opposing forces to the north and south of Israel. So, we can expect today to see two regional powers developing: one to the north and one to the south of Israel. These powers will be hostile to one another. In other words, we can expect a coming neo-Seleucid Kingdom in the area covered by Turkey, Syria, Iraq, Lebanon, Iran; and a coming neo-Ptolemaic Kingdom in the area covered by Egypt, Libya, Sudan. And there'll be intermittent military conflict between these two regional powers which will have major implications for Israel. At present, it looks as if it's shaping up as an Islamic conflict. The current Syrian war pitches southern-funded (Sunni) opposition against northern-aligned (Shia) powers. But then verse 40 and the following verses add a further dimension:

"At the end time the king of the South will collide with him, and the king of the North will storm against him with chariots, with horsemen and with many ships; and he will enter countries, overflow them and pass through. He will also enter the Beautiful Land, and many countries will fall; but these will be rescued out of his hand: Edom, Moab and the foremost of the sons of Ammon. Then he will stretch out his hand against other countries, and the land of Egypt will not escape. But he will gain control over the hidden treasures of gold and silver and over all the precious things of Egypt; and Libyans and Ethiopians will follow at his heels. But rumors from the East and from the North will disturb him, and he will go forth with great wrath to destroy and annihilate many. He will pitch the tents of his royal pavilion between the seas and the beautiful Holy Mountain; yet he will come to his end, and no one will help him" (Daniel 11:40-45).

First of all, let's be clear: this invasion has no correspondence to historical facts - so it's still to happen. The events in verses 40-45 will take place at the time of the end, that is, they will occur in the second half of the 70th 'seven' of the program Gabriel showed as belonging to Daniel's people. Here, in verse 40, the king of the north and the king of the south both collide and storm against "the king who does as he pleases" (v.40). It's as if, latterly, the 'revived' Antichrist – the king who does as he pleases - seems to be no longer "the king of the north" (of v.40).

In verses (vv. 40-45) every occurrence of 'he' (seven times), 'him' (four times), and 'his' (three times) refers to "the king who does as he pleases" (v.36). He'll have entered into a covenant with the people of Israel, binding that nation as a part of his domain (Daniel 9:27). Any attack, then, against the land of Israel will be an attack against him with whom Israel is then joined by covenant. So, the king of the South and the king of the North will fight against the Antichrist. Israel will be occupied and many Jews will flee, seeking shelter among the Gentile nations.

When the Antichrist hears of the joint invasion by southern and northern forces, he'll move his army, sweeping through many countries like a flood (v.40). He'll move quickly into the land of Israel, 'the Beautiful Land' (v.41). His first strike will be against Egypt (Daniel 11:42-43a), for Egypt and her Arab allies (Libyans and Nubians, v.43) are the ones who will initiate the invasion on Israel. On this occasion the king will not conquer the territory of Edom, Moab, and Ammon (v.41), nowadays included in the present kingdom of Jordan.

Then the Antichrist will hear alarming reports from the east (probably referring to an invasion by a massive army of two hundred million soldiers from east of the Euphrates River - see Revelation 9:16) and from the north (perhaps another attack by the king of the North). Enraged, the Antichrist will set out to destroy many of the invaders. Then he'll occupy Israel and pitch his royal tents between the seas, that is, between the Dead Sea and the Mediterranean Sea, at the beautiful holy mountain, probably

Brian Johnston

Jerusalem. The duration of Daniel's last-mentioned king has been determined by God.

How are things shaping up today? Well, I'd suggest you keep your eyes on Turkey. It's within the bounds of what was the Seleucid empire. And don't forget that the Ottoman empire (the previous expression of the Islamic Caliphate) was Turkish. Both Isaiah and Micah in the Bible repeatedly speak of opposition to the people of the Messiah which comes from 'the Assyrian.' Historically (say, 650 BC), Assyria was largely composed of Turkey, Syria and Iraq.

"Now at that time Michael, the great prince who stands guard over the sons of your people, will arise. And there will be a time of distress such as never occurred since there was a nation until that time; and at that time your people, everyone who is found written in the book, will be rescued. Many of those who sleep in the dust of the ground will awake, these to everlasting life, but the others to disgrace and everlasting contempt. Those who have insight will shine brightly like the brightness of the expanse of heaven, and those who lead the many to righteousness, like the stars forever and ever. But as for you, Daniel, conceal these words and seal up the book until the end of time; many will go back and forth, and knowledge will increase" (Daniel 12:1-4).

What Daniel sealed up in his book, is revealed with the opening of the seals of the scroll received by Christ in Revelation. The duration of Daniel's last-mentioned king has been determined by God. He'll be successful as the world ruler during the time of unparalleled 'distress,' the three and one-half years of the Great Tribulation (see Matthew 24), being the second half of the 70th 'seven' of God's program for Daniel's people, the Jews. At the end of the 70th 'seven' all true Israelites will be rescued from the clutches of the Antichrist (Romans 11:26). Then 'the first resurrection' (Revelation 20) will take place – it's first in regard to the one thousand-year earthly kingdom which the Lord Jesus will set up at that time. (The establishment of Messiah's millennial kingdom will perhaps take place after an interval of 75 days, Daniel 12:12, during which the attack of Ezekiel 38 and 39 may take place as Israel are only then restored from the sword, living securely, and with the LORD in their midst).

When we watch the daily news, surely we can only conclude that the time is short! The vital question then must be: 'Are we ready for the Master?'

CHAPTER TWELVE STUDY QUESTIONS

1. What is the relevance of Isaiah 42:8-9 to these chapters?
2. In your own words, sketch out how the content of the book of Revelation fits into Daniel's predictive outline for Israel.
3. What's the latest update on events taking shape both to the north and south of Israel?
4. What is the book referred to in v.1?
5. What is the significance of the command to Daniel to 'seal the words of the scroll' in v.5?

About the Publisher

Hayes Press (www.hayespress.org) is a registered charity in the United Kingdom, whose primary mission is to disseminate the Word of God, mainly through literature. It is one of the largest distributors of gospel tracts and leaflets in the United Kingdom, with over 100 titles and hundreds of thousands despatched annually.

Hayes Press also publishes Plus Eagles Wings, a fun and educational Bible magazine for children, six times a year and Golden Bells, a popular daily Bible reading calendar in wall or desk formats.

Also available are over 100 Bibles in many different versions, shapes and sizes, Christmas cards, Christian jewellery, Eikos Bible Art, Bible text posters and much more!